# A Workbook for Improving Your Health

Finding What Needs Attention,
1504 Homeopathic Remedies, 39 Bach
Flower Remedies and Chakras

Leonidas Wolf, Ph.D.

© 2017 Leonidas Wolf

**3**

## Table of Contents

DISCLAIMER ............................................................................... 7
INTRODUCTION. Introductory Pendulum Questions, Testing and "Chart B1" ................................................................................ 13
INTRODUCTION. Introductory Pendulum Questions, Testing and "Chart B1" ................................................................................ 13
............................................................................................... 16
***** PART 1. UNIVERSAL PENDULUM CHARTS .......... 16
CHAPTER 1. Simple Yes-No Answers (A4) ............................. 17
CHAPTER 2. Yes-No-Maybe and probabilities (A1) ............... 18
CHAPTER 3. Numbers – Answers (A2) ................................... 20
CHAPTER 4. Letters –Answers (A3) ....................................... 23
CHAPTER 5. Questions which could not be Answered (S1) .... 25
............................................................................................... 27
***** PART 2. WHAT NEEDS ATTENTION ....................... 27
CHAPTER 6. Balance of Energies ............................................ 29
CHAPTER 7. Major factors Influencing Health (Chart C3) .... 30
CHAPTER 7. Major factors Influencing Health (Chart C3) .... 30
   Description of Chakras ........................................................ 32
   Symptoms of Energy Blockages in Chakras ....................... 34
   Aura Balancing .................................................................... 36
CHAPTER 7. Rating of the Identified Issues (C2) ................... 38
CHAPTER 8. Human Anatomy – Body Systems (C4) ............. 40
   Body Systems ...................................................................... 40
............................................................................................... 42
***** PART 3. REMEDIES ...................................................... 42
CHAPTER 9. Bach Flower Remedies ....................................... 43
   Category 1. Fear .................................................................. 44
   Category 2. Uncertainty ...................................................... 44
   Category 3. Disinterest in Current Circumstances .............. 45
   Category 4. Loneliness ........................................................ 45
   Category 5. Oversensitivity to Ideas .................................. 45
   Category 6. Despondency and Despair ............................... 46
   Category 7. Overly Concerned about Others' Welfare ......... 47
   How to use Bach flower remedies: ...................................... 49
CHAPTER 11. Homeopathic Remedies. ................................... 50
CHAPTER 12. Miscellaneous Pendulum Readings. ................. 53

APPENDIX A. Human Anatomy .................................................. 55
   A. Digestive system ................................................................. 55
   B. Respiratory system ............................................................. 55
   C. Urinary system ................................................................... 55
   D. Female reproductive system ............................................... 56
   E. Male reproductive system .................................................. 56
   F. Endocrine glands ................................................................ 56
   G. Circulatory system ............................................................. 56
   H. Lymphatic system .............................................................. 57
   I. Nervous system .................................................................... 57
   J. Peripheral nervous system .................................................. 57
   K. Sensory organs ................................................................... 57
   L. Integumentary system (skin and its appendages) ............... 58
   M. Main Body Systems .......................................................... 58
APPENDIX B. Nosodes and Sarcodes. ....................................... 59
APPENDIX C. Schedule-calendar for Homeopathic Remedies. 66
APPENDIX D. Full List of Homeopathic Remedies, Numbered
............................................................................................................ 68
   A ------------------------ ................................................................. 68
   B ------------------------ ................................................................. 73
   C ------------------------ ................................................................. 75
   D ------------------------ ................................................................. 81
   E ------------------------ ................................................................. 82
   F ------------------------ ................................................................. 83
   G ------------------------ ................................................................. 84
   H ------------------------ ................................................................. 86
   I ------------------------ ................................................................. 87
   J ------------------------ ................................................................. 88
   K ------------------------ ................................................................. 89
   L ------------------------ ................................................................. 90
   M ------------------------ ................................................................. 91
   N ------------------------ ................................................................. 94
   O ------------------------ ................................................................. 95
   P ------------------------ ................................................................. 96
   Q ------------------------ ................................................................. 100
   R ------------------------ ................................................................. 100
   S ------------------------ ................................................................. 101
   T ------------------------ ................................................................. 105

    U ........................................................................ 107
    V ........................................................................ 107
    W ....................................................................... 108
    X ........................................................................ 108
    Y ........................................................................ 109
    Z ........................................................................ 109
APPENDIX E. Pendulum Charts ............................................. 110
    CHART B1.  Starting Point and Introductory Questions ...... 111
    CHART A1.  Yes-No-Maybe and Probabilities ................... 112
    CHART A2.  Digits 1 – 9 and Decimal Point ..................... 113
    CHART A3.  Letters ............................................................ 114
    CHART S1.  Problems with the Answers ........................... 115
    CHART A4.  Simple Yes-No ............................................... 116
    CHART "0 to 10" .................................................................. 117
    CHART "0 to 100" ................................................................ 118
    CHART "0 to 1000" .............................................................. 119
    CHART C1.  What Needs Attention ..................................... 120
    CHART C1a.  Main Areas of Life ......................................... 121
    CHART C1b.  Chakras ......................................................... 122
    CHART C2. Severity of a Condition or Situation ................ 123
    CHART C3.  General Issues ................................................ 124
    CHART C4.  Body Systems ................................................ 125
    CHART C5.  Categories of Bach Flower Remedies ............ 126
    CHART C6.  Selecting Potencies in Homeopathy .............. 127
    CHART C7.  Number of Days to the Next Remedy ............. 128

# DISCLAIMER

All the information provided in this book, and references to resource materials, are not intended to diagnose, treat, cure or prevent any disease condition or malady. No warranty is made or given that any information on or linked to this site is complete and/or accurate, and no warranty is given that there may not be a contrary view to any of the material that is hereby published. The information contained in this book, or obtained as a consequence of using this book, is not intended to be, nor is it implied to be, a substitute for professional medical or pharmaceutical advice. All book users should always seek the advice of their physician, pharmacist, or other qualified health care provider prior to commencing any new treatment for any of the conditions diseases or maladies in relation to which advice is sought through this book, and questions in relation to such treatment should be directed to your own such professional health care providers.

NOTHING CONTAINED IN THIS BOOK IS INTENDED TO BE NOR CAN IT BE TAKEN FOR MEDICAL DIAGNOSIS OR TREATMENT.

The contents of this book are offered as an information only, and are not compiled by a person or persons who are entitled directly or indirectly to practice medicine or dispense pharmaceuticals or medical services, nor do the information providers and/or author of this book dispense such information. The information providers and the author assume no warranty or liability whatsoever of any kind for the information and data contained in this book or for any diagnosis or treatment made while relying on this book. The information compiled by the information providers and contained in this book is in summary form only and is intended to provide broad consumer understanding and knowledge of pendulum dowsing. The information must not be considered complete, and should not be used in place of a consultation with or receipt of advice from a physician, pharmacist, or other health care provider. This book does not recommend or promote self management of health problems.

Information obtained by using this book is not exhaustive, and does not cover all diseases, conditions or maladies nor does it advise in relation to all possible treatments available for those diseases, conditions or maladies. Users are strongly advised to consult with their own physician, pharmacist or other health care provider, should their condition so require. Advice furnished by a qualified physician, pharmacist or health care provider should never be disregarded, nor should any delay occur in seeking a competent and qualified medical advice as a consequence of reading anything contained in this book.

The information contained in this book is based on various sources. These sources can be obtained from other books and the publicly available information. The author of this book is no more responsible for the information contained in the book, than is the custodian of information contained in a public library, as this book provides a convenient source of information collation, and no more.

THEREFORE, ALL INFORMATION SUPPLIED IN THIS BOOK HAS NO WARRANTY WHATSOEVER.

Users are therefore reminded to seek professional advice in relation to each particular disease, condition or malady from which the user may suffer, and to check with a physician, pharmacist or health care provider in relation to the correct treatment and/or dosages required to treat, control or cure such disease, condition or malady.

AS THE BOOK READER, YOU TAKE FULL AND TOTAL RESPONSIBILITY FOR WHAT YOU DO WITH THE INFORMATION PROVIDED IN THIS BOOK, AND ANY RESULTING OUTCOMES FROM YOUR ACTIONS.

No party or entity associated with this book, a related website and/or information, will take any responsibility at all for what you do with this information, what happens to you or any other person or party as a result of any information found or read or the validity or accuracy of any information contained or leaked from this book.

All care is taken in relation to ensuring that information furnished by the author of this book is as up to date as is possible. No responsibility is accepted if any of the information sought by users is subsequently found to be out of date or superseded.

THIS DISCLAIMER COVERS ALL MATERIAL INFORMATION OF ALL TYPES IN ANY AND EVERY PART OF THIS BOOK, ITS ATTACHMENTS AND THE RELATED WEBSITE.

# THE PURPOSE OF THIS BOOK

This book will guide you to healing, using the truth-finding powers of your pendulum. You will be guided, starting from training your pendulum, to finding which areas of your life need attention and improvement or healing. The charts in this book will help you to find out the root causes of any present or potential problems, which could affect your health. In addition to detailed localization of trouble points in your body, the pendulum may point you to the sources of stress or other negative influences, such as toxins, financial worries or environmental factors.

Some pendulum reading charts in this book are very general, which will permit you to find remedies far beyond those, which are listed in the book. Practically, any available and enumerated listing of remedies or symptoms can be investigated with the use of the Numbers or Letters Charts from this book. Be creative and use the lists relevant to your needs.

Pendulum will enable you to find out which one, out of 1504 homeopathic remedies listed in this book, will be the best for you. The advantage of pendulum over standard methods of searching for homeopathic remedies (repertorization) is that your pendulum is capable to evaluate even little known remedies, for which the repertory books usually have insufficient information. If a little known remedy is a perfect fit for you, your pendulum will find it out.

The pendulum charts in this book do not have ambiguities, as in other books about pendulums. For example, in some other books, which use an 180° semi-circle, the lines indicating Yes and No are extensions of each other. With this colinearity, finding what is the true answer is likely to be incorrect in 50% of the cases! While pendulum is not likely to be correct in all the cases, a reasonable estimate of the accuracy of a pendulum is about 95% accuracy. The accuracy increases with practice. The pendulum used by the author of this book is claiming 99% accuracy! Ask your pendulum about its accuracy and monitor if it is improving with time.

The graphs used in this book are not ambiguous, because they were designed in such a way that the angular difference between the lines is at least 20°, and the fan-like graphs use only 140° angular space of the full circle. All the graphs in this book were designed by the author, with the avoidance of ambiguity in mind. To achieve high accuracy for difficult readings, such as finding the best remedy out of 1504 listed, a two or three step procedure is used in this book, where in each step, the list of potential candidate remedies is narrowed down.

While homeopathy is the main healing method promoted in this book, this book has also chapters dedicated to the easy to use Bach flower remedies. Charts for chakra testing are also included, with the chakra balancing described in the text.

With respect to remedies, in this book the preference was given to homeopathic remedies, because they are powerful, low cost, all potencies are available over the counter, and the author of this book is using them with very good results. It may be interesting to note, that the royal family in the United Kingdom uses homeopaths and the homeopathic remedies.

The country which leads the world in the discipline of homeopathy is now India, with such prominent people as Rajan Shankaran, Kalyan Banerjee or Farokh Master. Homeopaths from other parts of the world travel to India for training.

# INTRODUCTION. Introductory Pendulum Questions, Testing and "Chart B1"

To work with this book you will need a pendulum. A pointed pendulum is preferred for the charts in this book, as an accurate alignment with the lines on the chart will need to be observed. To avoid any ambiguity, all the lines on the charts in this book are making an angle with the horizontal base. Charts in several other books about the use of pendulum have lines of one meaning aligned with lines of another meaning, which reduces accuracy, as the Yes answer can be easily taken for No. All the charts in this book were prepared by the author.

Always have a friendly attitude toward your pendulum. While training your pendulum, remember that the training is for you as well. In answering questions, your pendulum can demonstrate an incredible intelligence, so have respect for it. The other aspect of pendulum is that it does not recognize metaphors and takes every word literally. For example, do not use the word "cool" in the meaning that something will look very good. The words in the questions have to be simple, precise and without any slightest ambiguity.

The very first action in pendulum readings is to train pendulum to provide you with the YES and NO answers. You do this by deliberately moving pendulum as in chart B1, saying: "Pendulum, this is the YES answer". Keep training the pendulum with the remaining answers from the Yes-No Chart. Once you have trained your pendulum, check some obvious information, such as: "Is today Friday?" or "Is my last name Smith?" The answers should be correct. With the remaining charts, just ask the pendulum if it accepts the chart for providing the answers.

Pendulum will not be permitted or may not want to answer some questions. In these cases, the pendulum will send you to "Chart S1", which will indicate the problem, such as "The question is ambiguous" or "Wrong time to ask this question". The "not permitted" questions depend on the individual querent. For example, some people will not be permitted to know about their past lives.

At this point, you can go to Chart B1 and start training your pendulum. Then, formulate your first question and proceed through Chart B1 to make sure that the reading for the first question and the readings for the further questions will be correct. The full-scale Chart B1 is located in the Appendix. For your work, use the full-size Chart B1. A reduced version of **the Chart B1** is shown below, for your orientation.

## CHART B1 STARTING POIN 
### Introductory Questions

- <u>Please confirm that:</u>
  * I may ask the question as written, <u>or</u> carry out the action as written <u>and</u>
  * You are willing to answer it correctly, a 
  * The answer or the action will be benefi 
  and my family and not harmful to othe 

Once you have completed CHART B1, you can ask your pendulum if it will accept other charts in this book. Do it for each individual chart, starting from the CHART A1 and proceeding to A2, A3, A4, S1, C1, C2, C3 C4 etc. Charts A1, A2, A3, and S1 are very useful in finding hidden problems and appropriate remedies.

You can also create your own charts from the provided Blank Charts or even by drawing lines similar to those in Chart S1. I suggest using a ruler for drawing the lines, as pendulum likes straight lines.

## ***** PART 1. UNIVERSAL PENDULUM CHARTS

The A-series charts (A1 to A4), are universal and are applicable to finding solutions to nearly all possible questions. Since this book is about health improvement, detailed lists and special charts were created, to facilitate finding information related specifically to your health improvement.

You can use the universal pendulum charts to get answers to the questions far beyond the subject of improving your health, such as relationships, finances, investing, business and rating of various options.

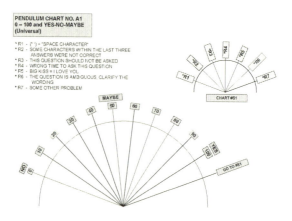

# CHAPTER 1. Simple Yes-No Answers (A4)

The simple Yes-No Answers are very convenient, because you can get these answers in almost any situation, with no need to have a pendulum-reading chart.

In the Introduction section of this book you have trained your pendulum on the Simple Yes-No chart. This training is important, because now you can ask your pendulum if it will accept additional charts for getting more insight into your situations.

From time to time, you should repeat going through the questions in the B1 Chart to assure that your pendulum is working well for you. Also, remember about testing your pendulum using such simple questions as: "Is today Friday?"

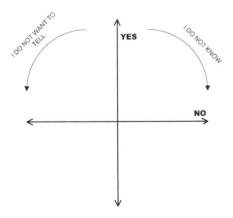

The full size version of this Chart is located in the Attachments section.

# CHAPTER 2. Yes-No-Maybe and probabilities (A1)

The Yes-No-Maybe Chart in this book is more accurate than the "Simple Yes-No Chart". "Chart A1" has a scale, and can provide answers about probability of events or situations. The scale of the probabilities is from "0" to "100", so it also provides a numerical estimate on the Maybe answer. The numerical "Maybe" answers can be quite informative. For example, the answer: "80", will mean "maybe, but most likely yes", while the answer "30" will mean "maybe, but most likely no". Therefore, this chart provides a way of rating the Maybe answers, which may prove useful in rating options which will appear as being similar.

The probability of future events and actions can be found using Chart A1. An example of such a question is: "What is the probability that [ *event* ...... ] will happen? The answer from your pendulum will be in the percentages of probability.

If there is a problem with the answer, the Pendulum will indicate, "Go to Chart S1". The S1 Chart provides hints explaining why the pendulum refused to give an answer. There are some questions, which should not be asked, and your pendulum will refuse to answer those questions.

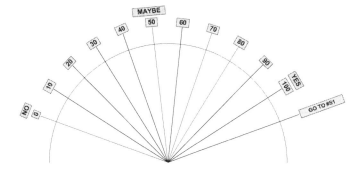

The full size version of this Chart is located in the Attachments section.

# CHAPTER 3. Numbers – Answers (A2)

The "Numbers Chart" provides answers as numbers, from single digit numbers to very large numbers and even fractional numbers.

This chart is extremely useful, as it provides a quick way to search large lists of areas of interest. The lists can be used to find out which part of the body requires attention. It can also lead to finding homeopathic remedies, Bach flower remedies or some other actions to improve your health.

This book makes an intense use of the "Numbers" chart for the selection of items from the large lists. The pendulum operates by getting answers from your subconscious mind. Your subconscious mind has access to the same source of information, as clairvoyants, psychics, and autistic savants. The autistic savants have incredible capacities in some narrow fields, such as music or calculations.

For the pendulum, to work properly in finding answers, you need to do the following:
1. Formulate your question. The best way is to write it down on paper.

2. Open and turn the pages with the list from which you will get the answer. Quickly glance at the whole list; you do not need to read it. Your subconscious mind will grasp the information.

3. Find out how many digits you will need in your numerical answer. It should be no more than three digits, as even the largest list of homeopathic remedies was split into sections based on the first letter of the name of the homeopathic remedy. For some lists, such as the large homeopathic remedy list, you will first have to go to the "Letters Chart", to get the first letter of the remedy. This first letter will guide you to a subsection of the whole list. From that subsection you will find out how many digits you need there.

4. Read the digits from the Numbers Chart and find the answer from the list. The page numbers for the first letters you can find out in the Table of Contents. For homeopathy you may need to ask for three remedies, as a single remedy is rarely sufficiently holistic to fit all your symptoms. With homeopathy, the next step will be to find out about the potency of the found remedies. Once you will get the potency of the remedy, write the information down. At this point verify that the information gained so far is correct: ask the pendulum if each of the found remedies, with their specific potencies, will be beneficial to you.

The reduced version of the "Numbers Chart" is below; the full version is included in the Attachments.

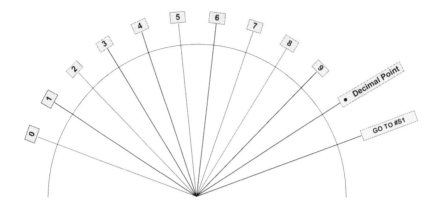

# CHAPTER 4. Letters –Answers (A3)

In this book, the pendulum chart for finding letters is used to find subsections of the large lists. Letters are convenient, as one chart with letters permits finding one of 26 potential answers. There are 26 letters in the English alphabet. After finding the letter corresponding to a subsection, the large list is investigated further using the numbers chart. Up to three digits for one number are used in this book. The pendulum chart for finding letters can also be used for finding names.

The procedure for the "Letters Chart" is a two-stage procedure, slightly different than for the other charts. It is as follows:

1. Put the pendulum in the center of the large circle and ask the pendulum for the first letter of the subsection in the list that you are investigating. The pendulum will indicate a group of three letters.

2. Put the pendulum in the place on the circumference of the large circle, where the lines lined to the found three letters intersect. From that point start a new reading for the one of the three letters.

The reduced version of the "Letters Chart" is below; the full version is included in the Attachments.

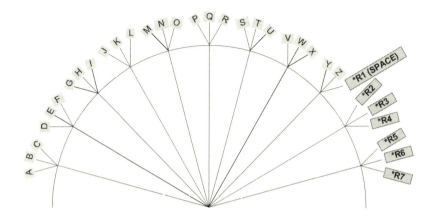

# CHAPTER 5. Questions which could not be Answered (S1)

Pendulum may refuse to provide answers to some questions. The "not answered questions" are usually in the category of questions about the past lives or karma.

Almost all the charts have an option of sending the reader to the supplementary chart, which in this book is called the "S1 Chart".

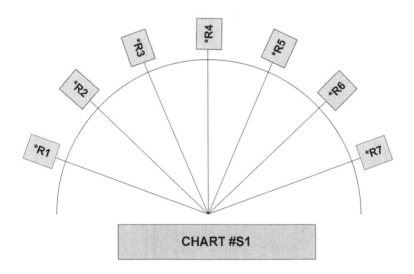

* R1 - (" ") = "SPACE CHARACTER"
* R2 - SOME CHARACTERS WITHIN THE LAST THREE ANSWERS WERE NOT CORRECT
* R3 - THIS QUESTION SHOULD NOT BE ASKED
* R4 - WRONG TIME TO ASK THIS QUESTION

* R5  -  BIG KISS = I LOVE YOU
* R6  -  THE QUESTION IS AMBIGUOUS, CLARIFY THE WORDING
* R7  -  SOME OTHER PROBLEM

## \*\*\*\*\* PART 2. WHAT NEEDS ATTENTION

This part concentrates on finding areas in your general environment, which requires attention. These areas include:
- your energies (physical, mental, emotional and spiritual),
- major factors influencing your health (environment, nutrition, stress and emotional aspects),
- chakras,
- aura balancing,
- nutrition, vitamins and hormones,
- toxins,
- allergies and
- infections.

The chapters that
  The chapters that are included in Part 2 of this book are discussing the above listed factors.

are included in Part 2 of this book are discussed in the chapters that follow this brief introduction.

# CHAPTER 6. Balance of Energies

You can use **Chart C1a,** to find out which of your energies, such as physical, mental, emotional or spiritual, need attention. **Chart C1a** analyzes the highest levels of factors that affect your life. Proceed with rating the needs using **Chart C2** (Severity of Situation or Condition").

**Chart C3** in Chapter 7 (the next chapter) analyzes factors influencing your health from a different point of view.

Chart C1a, reduced (below):

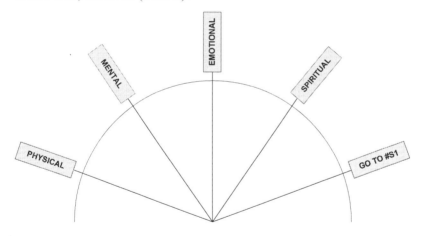

# CHAPTER 7. Major factors Influencing Health (Chart C3)

**Chart C3** takes a "bird's view" on <u>major factors</u> which could be troublesome to your health and other vital issues. Use this Chart to find out which areas need attention. **Chart C3** combines the Letters Chart and the list of factors influencing health, from below this paragraph. If you prefer to work with the Numbers Chart, you can use the "stand alone" Numbers Chart with the list of the factors provided below this paragraph. For the Numbers Chart you can use a two-step procedure, using the digits "0 to 9", to identify the two digits corresponding to the issue. Once the issues are identified, proceed with rating them, using **Chart C2** (Severity of Situation or Condition").

**List of the major factors influencing health:**

A. 01. Miasms
B. 02. Subconscious beliefs
C. 03. Love and relationships
D. 04. Chakras
E. 05. Meridians
F. 06. Aura
G. 07. Energies
H. 08. Entities
I. 09. Environment
J. 10. Stress
K. 11. Hormones
L. 12. Vitamins
M. 13. Nutrition
N. 14. Minerals

N. 15. Electrolytes
O. 16. Toxins
P. 17. Allergies
Q. 18. Infections
R. 19. Disorders

The "Letters reading part of Chart C3", reduced (below):

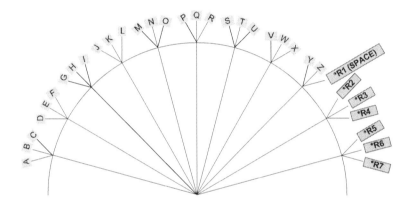

# CHAPTER 8. Chakras (Chart C1b)

For thousands of years, chakras were recognized as the nodes of the flow of the vital energy in people. The vital energy is known in different cultures as "vis vitalis" (Europe), "Chi" (Far East), "Mana" (Hawaiian Islands) etc. Clairvoyants can see the chakras as spinning, multi-petal "lotus flowers", with each chakra having its own color and a specific number of petals. Chakras, and the energy blockages within chakras, can be sensed using the pendulum.

## *Description of Chakras*

### #1. The Root Chakra

The root chakra is red, four-petal, and it is situated at the base of the spine. This chakra transfers universal energies into the physical level. It is related to the earth element. It is also related to the anus, rectum, colon, prostate gland and the spine.

### #2. The Sacral Chakra

The sacral chakra is orange, six-petal, and is situated at the level of the sacrum in the back of the body. It is related to the water element. The sacral chakra influences emotional balance, and sexual life. It is related to the reproductive system.

### #3. The Solar Chakra

The solar chakra is yellow, ten-petal, and it is located near the solar plexus. It is related to the fire element. It influences emotions. In the body, it influences the digestive system and the lower back.

## #4. The Heart Chakra

The heart chakra is green, twelve-petal, situated in line center of the chest, at the heart level. It is related to the air Element. It controls understanding, love and empathy. In the body it is related to the heart, lungs, and upper back.

## THE TRINITY

**The three top chakras** are known as the trinity.

## #5. The Throat Chakra

The throat chakra is blue, sixteen-petaled, and is located in the throat. It controls communication between the brow chakra and the lower ones, so it is a bridge between our thoughts and feelings. In the body it is related to respiration, the neck, ears, and arms.

## #6. The Brow Chakra (The Third-Eye Chakra)

The brow chakra is indigo in color, has ninety-six-petals and is located in the forehead, between the eyebrows. It regulates the mind, thought, and intuition. In the body it is related to the thinking processes and regulates the sinuses.

#7. The Crown Chakra

The crown chakra is chakra is violet, thousand-petaled, and located slightly above the head. The crown chakra controls all the energies of the other six chakras. It has connection with the Infinite Intelligence.

## *Symptoms of Energy Blockages in Chakras*

**Root chakra:** haemorrhoids, constipation, and prostate problems.
**Sacral chakra**: impotence, frigidity, menstrual problems, problems with the kidneys or gallbladder.
**Solar chakra:** eating disorders, ulcers.
**Heart chakra:** angina, hypertension.
**Throat chakra:** sore throats, problems with the voice.
**Brow chakra:** headaches, fuzzy or illogical thinking.
**Crown chakra:** loneliness, isolation, inability to see other people's points of view.

You can use your pendulum to determine the well-being of each individual chakra using **Chart C1b**.

**Chart C1b, reduced, below:**

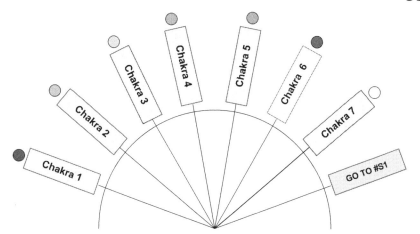

## *Aura Balancing*

Aura balancing is a simple process that has the power to remove blockages from the chakras and bring perfect health to the people. Use **Chart C1b** to analyze yours the chakras of your own or even chakras of other people.

The first question to ask is: "Which one of my chakras is the most malfunctioning". Then, ask if any other chakra could also benefit from the balancing.

One way of removing the negative energies from a chakra is to move them into a cup of water containing a pinch of some sea-salt. Keep the pendulum in your prominent hand and immerse the fingers of the other hand in the cup's water.
Suspend your pendulum over the image of the chakra to be balanced and ask the pendulum to remove all negative
energies from that chakra. The pendulum will start moving in the direction that indicates negative energies. The negative energies

will be coming up to the pendulum, and will pass through your arm, your chest, and down into the glass of water.

When the pendulum stops moving, take your fingers out of the water and wash your hands under running water.

Continue the process with other out-of-balance chakras. Once the balancing is completed, do a follow-up check, using the pendulum, to find out if each chakra gives positive reading. Repeat the process if there is some residual negativity.

**The blockages in the chakras cause the following problems:**

1. **Root chakra:** insecurity, self-doubt, deliberating the past mistakes.

2. **Sacral chakra:** selfishness, problems with effective communication with others.

3. **Solar chakra:** low self-esteem, feelings of having no power.

4. **Heart chakra:** problems in expressing emotions, hiding your feelings, lack of empathy.

5. **Throat chakra:** Problems with expressing yourself and problems with expressing your emotions.

6. **Brow chakra:** daydreaming.

7. **Crown chakra:** Feelings of being alienated from others. Lack of flexibility in thinking about the future.

# CHAPTER 7. Rating of the Identified Issues (C2)

The condition of the issue needing attention can be rated on a numerical scale from 0 to 9. The higher the value, the better the condition. Low values indicate that some action has to be taken, as in the listing below.

The "0 to 9" scale can rate the health issues, identified in Charts C3 and C4, as well as other areas of your life or of your interest.

**The ratings are as follows:**

0. Very severe condition, needs an urgent intervention
1. Significant problem, needs quick intervention
2. Medium problem, needs intervention, no rush
3. Some minor problem, it may go away on its own
4. Needs attention, problems may develop in a month
5. Borderline, but OK
6. Behaving properly
7. Good condition
8. Very good condition
9. Excellent condition

Chart C2, reduced, is shown below:

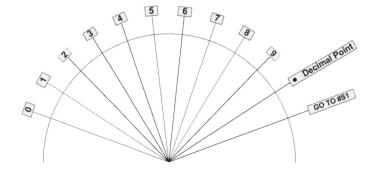

# CHAPTER 8. Human Anatomy – Body Systems (C4)

To analyze the body systems using pendulum use the following simple procedure:

1. Use the "Letters" Chart to find out which body system needs attention. Ask the pendulum if it will agree to provide you the information about your body part which needs attention. Normally, the pendulum will agree to provide this information. Then, go to the Chart C4, which has the Letters graph combined with the listing of the body systems. For example, the letter "B" will correspond to the respiratory system, as in the table below. The systems and their corresponding letters are listed below.
2. As a second step, use the "Numbers" Chart (A2) to get a sequence of numbers corresponding to the specific body part, as listed in Appendix A.

## *Body Systems*

| | |
|---|---|
| 1 | A. Digestive system |
| 2 | B. Respiratory system |
| 3 | C. Urinary system |
| 4 | D. Female reproductive system |
| 5 | E. Male reproductive system |
| 6 | F. Endocrine glands |
| 7 | G. Circulatory system |

| | |
|---|---|
| 8 | H. Lymphatic system |
| 9 | I. Nervous system |
| 10 | J. Peripheral nervous system |
| 11 | K. Sensory organs |
| 12 | L. Integumentary system (skin and its appendages) |
| 13 | M. Other body systems (skeleton, muscles etc.). |

The "Letters reading part of Chart C4", reduced, below:

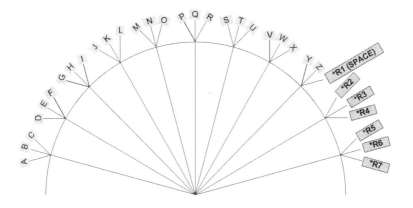

**Example:** If your reading will give you the following:
- the letter "B" and
- the digit "6",

then your lungs are the area which needs attention.

## \*\*\*\*\*  PART 3. REMEDIES

The chapters in this part will cover the Bach flower remedies and homeopathic remedies. The Bach flower remedies are very gentle, but they still can help with the issues which have emotional background. Homeopathy is a system which is also gentle, but is useful in a wide variety of health problems. Homeopathy is particularly useful in chronic problems, where allopathic medicine is generally of low effectiveness.

The Bach flower remedies are discussed in Chapter 11, and summarized in Chapter 13. Chapter 14 provides guidance for selection of homeopathic remedies using pendulum dowsing.

# CHAPTER 9. Bach Flower Remedies

Bach Flower Remedies are effective to restore emotional balance in people's lives. There are 38 "single flower" remedies, divided into seven categories. Use **Chart C5** to find the category of the flower remedy which will be helpful for you. Then, use the "Numbers Chart" to get a number corresponding to the identified category. As with other charts, you can get answers for other people as well.

After finding the category of the Bach flower remedy, get the number of the remedy from the "Numbers Chart". This way you will arrive at the right remedy.

Edward Bach classified his flowers into seven categories, as listed below:

    Category 1 - Fear
    Category 2 - Uncertainty
    Category 3 - Disinterest in Current Circumstances
    Category 4 - Loneliness
    Category 5 - Oversensitivity to Ideas
    Category 6 - Loss of Hope and Despair
    Category 7 - Overly concerned about Others' Welfare

The characteristics of the Bach Flower remedies are described below. The listing below also provides the numbers of the remedy, which can be identified in the way described above.

## *Category 1. Fear*

**1. Rock Rose.** For anxiety, fright and scary dreams.

**2. Mimulus.** For lack of confidence, phobias and anxiety.

**3. Cherry Plum.** For mood swings, and being close to losing control over person's behavior and feeling a "breakdown".

**4. Aspen.** For general anxiety.

**5. Red Chestnut.** For excessive worry and excessive concern about others.

## *Category 2. Uncertainty*

**1. Cerato.** For people who doubt their own abilities at making decisions.

**2. Scleranthus.** For difficulties in making decisions.

**3. Gentian.** For being easily discouraged.

**4. Gorse.** For feelings of being incompetent, hopelessness and in a state of despair.

**5. Hornbeam.** For procrastination, and avoiding taking on tasks.

**6. Wild Oat.** For people who are dissatisfied with their current lifestyle.

## Category 3. Disinterest in Current Circumstances

1. **Clematis.** For daydreaming and lack of interest in life.

2. **Honeysuckle.** For people who spend too much time and energy deliberating mistakes from the past.

3. **Wild Rose.** For people who are apathetic and believing that they cannot change their fate, which appears to be filled with troubles.

4. **Olive.** For people who have depleted themselves mentally and physically.

5. **White chestnut.** For being preoccupied with unwanted thoughts.

6. **Mustard.** For elimination sudden feelings of melancholy or sadness.

7. **Chestnut Bud.** For people who are repeating the same mistakes.

## Category 4. Loneliness

1. **Water Violet.** For people do not like to share their feelings.

2. **Impatiens.** For a strong impatience to other's responses.

3. **Heather.** For people who talk excessively and like to be with those who will listen to their talk.

## Category 5. Oversensitivity to Ideas

1. **Agrimony.** For people who keep their feelings strictly to themselves.

2. **Centaury.** For people who have problems to turn down the requests from others.

3. **Walnut.** For people who have problems with balancing their emotions during changes of circumstances.

4. **Holly.** For elimination of jealousy, suspicion and hate.

## Category 6. Despondency and Despair

1. **Larch.** For lack of trust in own abilities.

2. **Pine.** For people who believe that they are to be blamed for negative events happening around them.

3. **Elm.** For people who feel that the things which they need to do are overwhelming and much above their abilities.

4. **Sweet Chestnut.** To help overcome the feelings that the limits of endurance were exceeded for the person. People in despair.

5. **Star of Bethlehem**. To help with severe mental and emotional stress.

6. **Willow.** To help eliminate feelings of resentment and self-pity.

7. **Oak.** To help hard working people who never consider resting and work beyond the point of being exhausted.

8. **Crab Apple.** For people who dislike some aspects of their personality. Also, obsessive behaviors and feeling unclean.

## *Category 7. Overly Concerned about Others' Welfare*

1. **Chicory.** For people who want to keep their loved ones dependent and in close proximity.

2. **Vervain.** For people who feel a strong need to persuade other people to share their own point of view.

3. **Vine.** For people who think that they know what is best for others and expect obedience from others.
4. **Beech.** For people who are intolerant to irritable.

5. **Rock water.** For people who are rigid and carry on self-repression.

# CHAPTER 10. Summary of Bach Flower Remedies

The Bach flower remedies are listed in the Homeopathic Pharmacopeia of the United States (HPUS) and are quite similar to the liquid homeopathic remedies. The Bach's remedies are prepared at a 5x homeopathic dilution (0.01 mg of active substance per milliliter of tincture that is 10 ppm concentration). Like homeopathy and Reiki, the Bach Flower remedies are working at an energetic level in the body. This class of complementary therapies is usually called vibrational medicine.

Dr. Bach's intended to create a limited number of simple remedies, so the people could easily get familiar with his remedies, identify the correspondence between their negative emotions and his remedies, and help themselves in coping with those emotions. The number of Bach flower remedies is 38. From that number, 37 remedies are made from selected species of flowers, and one from special spring water.

Bach Flower remedies are used to eliminate or reduce the stress and other unpleasant emotional states of people or even animals. Through elimination of stress, the Bach remedies are contributing to maintenance of a healthy immune system.

For emotional crises, such as being emotionally shaken after an accident or after a bad news, Bach recommended the "Bach Rescue Remedy", to recover calmness in these situations. The best way is to use the Bach's remedies is to use them as single remedies, with the exception of the "Bach Rescue Remedy", which is a mixture formulated by Dr. Bach, himself.

There are 5 Bach Flower Remedies in the Rescue Remedy, all at the 5x dilution, in 27% grape-based alcohol or glycerine:
1. Star of Bethlehem,
2. Rock Rose,
3. Cherry Plum,
4. Impatiens,
5. Clematis.

## *How to use Bach flower remedies:*

1. Get a new, 30 mol bottle, with a dropper in the lid, from your local pharmacy.
2. Add two drops of the selected remedy to the bottle. If you are using a ready-made emergency formula ("Bach Rescue Remedy")then use four drops of this liquid.
3. Fill up the bottle with uncarbonized mineral water (do not use fizzling water).
4. Use four drops, from your bottle), under the tongue, four times per day.

An alternative way of using the Bach flower remedies is to dilute two drops of the selected remedy in a glass of water (or any other drink), and sip it gradually.

The Bach flower remedies are also called "Flower Essences", which is misleading, because they are 5x diluted, while the essential oils are prepared and sold as concentrated volatile oils, distilled from the plants. The Essential oils are not diluted.

# CHAPTER 11. Homeopathic Remedies.

Homeopathic remedies are very powerful. They are particularly useful for chronic conditions, where the standard Western medicine (also called Allopathic Medicine) is not very effective. Most of the homeopathic medications are acting through influencing the energy balances in the body. They just provide the subtle energies that the body needs to heal itself.

For the selection of homeopathic remedies using pendulum, this book provides the selection process in steps. The first step is to find out if a remedy could be found within the group of the most commonly used homeopathic medications, so called polycrests. The group of polycrests consists of about 70 remedies. The polycrests are numbered in this book (see Table below). The number corresponding to the required remedy can be found by reading the first and the second digit corresponding to the polycrest remedy from the "Numbers Chart".

Table – Homeopathic polycrest remedies.

| | |
|---|---|
| 1 | Apis mellifica |
| 2 | Argentium nitricum |
| 3 | Arnica |
| 4 | Arsenicum album |
| 5 | Belladonna |
| 6 | Bryonia |
| 7 | Calc carbonica |
| 8 | Calcium fluoricum |
| 9 | Cantharis |
| 10 | Carbo vegetabilis |
| 11 | Chamomilla |
| 12 | Cocculus |
| 13 | Euphrasia |
| 14 | Gelsemium |

| | |
|---|---|
| **15** | Graphites |
| **16** | Hepar sulphuricum |
| **17** | Hypericum |
| **18** | Ignatia |
| **19** | Kali phosphoricum |
| **20** | Lycopodium |
| **21** | Natrum muriaticum |
| **22** | Nux vomica |
| **23** | Phosphorus |
| **24** | Pulsatilla |
| **25** | Rhus toxicodendton (Rhus tox) |
| **26** | Ruta graveolens (Ruta grav) |
| **27** | Silicea |
| **28** | Sulphur |
| **29** | Thuja |

Once the remedy is identified, you should verify if it corresponds to the most important symptoms to be eliminated. Detailed description for the remedies can be found on the following website:
  http://www.abchomeopathy.com/homeopathy.htm
where the remedies are catalogues with detailed description.

The next step is to find the potency of the remedy. This can be done by using Chart C6 (Selection of Potencies for Homeopathic Remedies). In most cases, you will get a reading for potency 6 CH, 12 CH and 30 CH. If your reading will indicate a need for potency over 30CH then you should ask the pendulum if lower potencies will also be effective. Make sure to ask if the action of the homeopathic remedy will be gentle. Particular care has to be exercised with remedies based on potassium (Kali Carbonicum etc.), mercury (Mercurius …) and nosodes (nosodes are extracted from deactivated bacteria. Nosodes are extremely diluted. Many homeopaths do not prescribe mercury in any cases. Sarcodes are derived from healthy tissues and plants. Nosodes are typically used in potencies of 200 CH and higher). A full list of nosodes and sarcodes is included in Appendix B.

For the chronic cases, at least two remedies should be selected. They should be used intermittently. Repeating of the same remedy with the same potency is not recommended in homeopathy. The timing of the remedies can be found from Chart C7.

As a rule of thumb in classical homeopathy, potencies of 6CH can be used daily, 12 CH once per week to once per month, and the 30 CH typically once per month. Higher potencies, such as 200CH, are typically administered only once per treatment. Some people react strongly to homeopathic remedies, and they should be treated with low potencies. A chart for the selection of proper timing of homeopathic remedies is included as Chart C7.

# CHAPTER 12. Miscellaneous Pendulum Readings.

Pendulum can provide you with answers to a wide range of questions. Consider formulating your question in a clear way, that is in such a way, that the "YES" or "NO" answer will not be ambiguous. When a "MAYBE" answer is possible, then use the Universal Scale with ratings from 0 to 100.

* **Love - Attraction**
  Use the scale 0 - 100 (put the printout of the scale from below near the 0-100 CHART, write the scale directly on the Pendulum Chart or simply keep this book open on the page with the scale), so you will see both the Universal 0-100 Chart and the scale from below.
  The scale for ratings "from no-attraction to love" is this:
  ----------------------------------
  100 = Full Strength Love
    50 = Attraction
    20 = Friendship
      0 = Lack of interest
  ----------------------------------

* **Chakras** (this book has a special chart for reading chakras - see Chart C1b).

* **World** (latitude and longitude)

Latitude - use numerical scale (the Universal 0 to 100 Chart) to get the number in the range from 0 to 90.

Longitude - use numerical scale. Get the numbers, 0 - 360 as three digits, one by one, from the 0- 9 scale.

* **Physical direction** (looking for a lost object etc.)
Use the blank graph for this purpose. First ask if the target is within the angle of the "blank directions" in the Blank Chart.

* **Time**

Use the 0- 9 scale to get the date in a format YYYYMMDD; if the year is known and specified in the question then you can get the month in the format of "MM".

* **Decision Making**

Mark the blank chart with your options or enumerate the options from 0 to 9 (or a part of it, on a sheet of paper near the pendulum's graph), and use the 0-to-9 CHART.

* **Blank Chart**
Use it to design your own custom options, according to your needs.

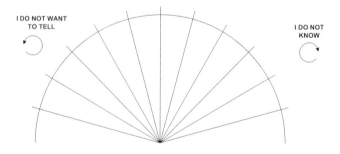

# APPENDIX A.  Human Anatomy

## A. *Digestive system*

1. Mouth  (general)
2. Teeth
3. Tongue
4. Salivary glands
5. Pharynx
6. Esophagus
7. Stomach
8. Small intestine
9. Large intestine
10. Liver
11. Gallbladder
12. Mesentery
13. Pancreas

## B. *Respiratory system*

1. Nasal cavity
2. Pharynx
3. Larynx
4. Trachea
5. Bronchi
6. Lungs
7. Diaphragm

## C. *Urinary system*

1. Kidneys
2. Ureters
3. Bladder
4. Urethra

## D. Female reproductive system

1. Ovaries
2. Fallopian tubes
3. Uterus
4. Vagina
5. Vulva
6. Clitoris
7. Placenta

## E. Male reproductive system

1. Testes
2. Epididymis
3. Vas deferens
4. Seminal vesicles
5. Prostate
6. Bulbourethral glands
7. Penis
8. Scrotum

## F. Endocrine glands

1. Pituitary gland
2. Pineal gland
3. Thyroid gland
4. Parathyroid glands
5. Adrenal glands
6. Pancreas

## G. Circulatory system

1. The heart
2. Arteries
3. Veins
4. Capillaries

## H. Lymphatic system

1. Lymphatic vessels
2. Lymph nodes
3. Bone marrow
4. Thymus
5. Spleen
6. Gut-associated lymphoid tissue
7. Tonsils

## I. Nervous system

1. The brain
2. Cerebrum
3. Diencephalon
4. The brainstem
5. Midbrain
6. Pons
7. Medulla oblongata
8. Cerebellum
9. The spinal cord
10. The ventricular system
11. Choroid plexus

## J. Peripheral nervous system

1. Cranial nerves
2. Spinal nerves
3. Ganglia
4. Enteric nervous system

## K. Sensory organs

1. Eye (in general)
2. Cornea
3. Iris
4. Ciliary body

5. Lens
6. Retina
7. Ear (in general)
8. Outer ear
9. Eardrum
10. Middle ear
11. Inner ear (in general)
12. Cochlea
13. Vestibule of the ear
14. Semicircular canals
15. Olfactory epithelium
16. Tongue
17. Taste buds

## L.  Integumentary system (skin and its appendages)

1. Mammary glands
2. Skin
3. Subcutaneous tissue

## M.  Main Body Systems

1. Human skeleton
2. Joints
3. Ligaments
4. Muscular system
5. Tendons

# APPENDIX B.  Nosodes and Sarcodes.

| | |
|---|---|
| 1 | Adrenalin (secretion of medulla of supra-renal gland) |
| 2 | Adrenocorticotrophin (from anterior pituitary gland of pigs) |
| 3 | Aorta |
| 4 | Arteria |
| 5 | Bulbinum |
| 6 | Cerebellum |
| 7 | Cerebellum cortex |
| 8 | Cholesterinum |
| 9 | Cholinum |
| 10 | Colon |
| 11 | Colostrum |
| 12 | Conjunctiva |
| 13 | Corpus luteum |
| 14 | Corticotropinum |
| 15 | Cortisone (steroid hormone from adrenal cortex of man) |
| 16 | Diaphragma |
| 17 | Discus invertebralis |
| 18 | D.N.A. |
| 19 | Duodenum |
| 20 | Fel tauri (ox gall) |
| 21 | Fel vulpis (fox gall) |
| 22 | Fibrinum |
| 23 | Folliculinum |
| 24 | Hemoglobinum |
| 25 | Hypothalamus |
| 26 | Insulin (beta cells of Islet of Langerhans of pancreas) |
| 27 | Labyrinthinum |

| | |
|---|---|
| 28 | Lac caninum |
| 29 | Lac felinum |
| 30 | Lac vaccinum |
| 31 | Liquor amnii |
| 32 | Luteinum |
| 33 | Lymphatica |
| 34 | Mamma |
| 35 | Meconium |
| 36 | Medulla ossea |
| 37 | Medulla spinalis |
| 38 | Mucosa nasalis |
| 39 | Myocardium |
| 40 | Nervus auditorius |
| 41 | Neurinum |
| 42 | Oophorinum (ovarian extract) |
| 43 | Orchitinum (testicular extract) |
| 44 | Pancreatinum (extract from pancreas of beef) |
| 45 | Parathyroid gland |
| 46 | Pepsinum (enzyme produced from stomach of sheep or calf) |
| 47 | Pituitaria glandula |
| 48 | Pituitaria glandula anterior |
| 49 | Pituitaria glandula posterior (posterior pituitary gland of sheep) |
| 50 | Placenta |
| 51 | Placenta suis |
| 52 | Prostata |
| 53 | Pulmo |
| 54 | Pulmo vulpis |
| 55 | Retina |
| 56 | R.N.A. |
| 57 | Secretinum |
| 58 | Serotoninum |
| 59 | Thyroidinum (healthy thyroid tissue of sheep or calf) |

| | |
|---|---|
| 60 | Thyroiodinum Some of the nosodes are questionable, for example: |
| 61 | Ambra grisea – discharge of the sperm whale. |
| 62 | Malaria officinalis – it is not a discharge but called a vegetable nosode. |
| 63 | Agaricus Muscaris – entire fresh fungus found in dry pinewoods. |
| 64 | Anthracinum - from the liver of rabbit suffering from Anthrax. |
| 65 | Anti-Colibacillary- caprine origin, made from goats immunized with E.coli. |
| 66 | Boletus Laricis- prepared from dried fungus Purging Agaric / Larch Boletus. |
| 67 | Botulinum- Clostridium Botulinum toxin made from putrefied pork. |
| 68 | Brucella Melintensis- a filtrate of the microbe of undulating fever. |
| 69 | Calculus bilialis |
| 70 | Calculus renalis- prepared from renal calculus. |
| 71 | Cholesterinum – prepared from gall stone. |
| 72 | Colibacillinum |
| 73 | Diphtherinum- diphtheria toxin; diphtheric membranes of a patient. |
| 74 | D.T.-T.A.B.- mixed vaccine of antidiphtheric, antitetanic and antitypho – paratyphoid. |
| 75 | Eberthinum- prepared from culture of mixture of many stocks of Salmonella typhi. |
| 76 | Enterococcinum- stocks of Streptococcus faecalis. |
| 77 | Flavus- prepared from Neisseria pharangis. |
| 78 | Gonotoxinum- prepared from anti Gonococcic vaccine. |
| 79 | Hippomanes- from the amniotic fluid of the mare. |
| 80 | Hippozaenium- lysate from the glander of horse. |
| 81 | Homarus |
| 82 | Hydrophobinum (Lyssin)- lysate of saliva taken |

|     | from a rabid dog. |
| --- | --- |
| 83  | Influenzinum virus A – stock prepared by Pasteur Institute |
| 84  | Influenzinum virus B – stock prepared by Pasteur Institute |
| 85  | Leprominum |
| 86  | Leprum |
| 87  | Leptospira- lysate of Leptospira ictero-haemorrhagie |
| 88  | Leusinum (Syphilinum)- prepared from syphilitic chancres. |
| 89  | Malandrinum- lysate from exudates of the horse malandra |
| 90  | Malaria Officinalis- prepared from mire taken during dryness of a malarial marsh. |
| 91  | Medorrhinum- discharge infected with Neisseria Gonorrhoeae. |
| 92  | Melitagrinum- nosode of Eczema capitis |
| 93  | Meningococcinum- prepared from stocks of Neisseria Meningitidis. |
| 94  | Monilia Albicans- lysate of culture of Monilia albicans |
| 95  | Morbillinum- from exudate of mouth and pharynx of measles affected patients |
| 96  | Mucor Mucedo- from the mushroom Mucor Mucedo |
| 97  | Mucotoxin |
| 98  | Nectrianinum- nosode of Cancer of trees. |
| 99  | Oscillococcinum- autolysate filtered from liver and heart of a duck. |
| 100 | Osteo Arthritis Nosode (O.A.N.)- synovial fluid of articulations especially knee and hip of osteoarthritic patients. |
| 101 | Ourlianum- lysate from the saliva of a patient suffering from mumps. |
| 102 | Paratyphoidinum- from cultures of different stocks of Paratyphoidinum bacilli. |
| 103 | Pertussinum- lysate from expectoration of patient |

| | |
|---|---|
| | suffering from whooping cough. |
| 104 | Pneumococcinum- Diplococcus pneumoniae found in saliva |
| 105 | Pneumotoxin- prepared from Diplococcus lanceolatus. |
| 106 | Psorinum- from serosity of furrows of itch of an unterated patient. |
| 107 | Pulmo anaphylacticus |
| 108 | Putrescinum |
| 109 | Pyrarara- lard of Pyrarara, a fish of the Amazon river. |
| 110 | Pyrogenum- prepared originally from decomposition of meat of beef. |
| 111 | Rheumatoid Arthritis Nosode (R.A.N)- from fluid of knee afflicted with rheumatoid arthritis |
| 112 | Sanguisuga- prepared from leech. |
| 113 | Scarlatinum- lysate from the scabs of a patient suffering from scarlatina. |
| 114 | Secale Cornutum- prepared from the fungus Claviceps purpura. |
| 115 | Serum of Yersin- from the anti-pest serum obtained from animals that have been immunized by means of live or killed cultures of Yersinia pestis. |
| 116 | Septicaeminum – prepared from septic abscess. |
| 117 | Sinusitisinum |
| 118 | Staphylococcinum- from Staphylococcus pyogenes aureus. |
| 119 | Staphylotoxinum- antitoxins of staphylococcus. |
| 120 | Streptococcinum- lysate obtained from stock of streptococcus. |
| 121 | Streptocnterococcinum- lysate of culture of strepto-enterococcus. |
| 122 | Tetanotoxinum – dilution of tetanic toxin. |
| 123 | Toxoplasma Gondii – lysate of Toxoplasma Gondii. |
| 124 | Ustilago Maydis- prepared from a fungus |

|     | growing on the Indian corn. |
| --- | --- |
| 125 | Usnea Barbata – prepared from lichen infecting soft maple. |
| 126 | Vaccin attenu bili |
| 127 | Vaccinotoxinum- prepared from anti-variolic vaccine. |
| 128 | Vaccinonum- prepared from the lymph of cowpox. |
| 129 | Variolinum- lysate obtained from the serosity of smallpox pustule. |
| 130 | Verriculum- prepared from warts. |
| 131 | Yersin (Pestinum)- nosode of plague. |
| 132 | Epitheliomine – extract of epithelioma. |
| 133 | Schirrinum- carcinoma schirrus (stomach). |
| 134 | Onkolysine- from a stock of Onkomyxa Neojormans. |
| 135 | Carcinosin-hepatica-metastat |
| 136 | Carcinosin laryngis |
| 137 | Carcinosin adenopapillary |
| 138 | Carcinosin adeno-stom- from adenocarcinoma of stomach. |
| 139 | Carcinosin adeno-vesica- papillary adenocarcinoma of bladder. |
| 140 | Carcinosin pulmonale- pulmonary cancer. |
| 141 | Carcinosin Schirr-mammae- schhirus of mammae. |
| 142 | Tuberculinum avis- prepared from Mycobacterium tuberculosis aviaire. |
| 143 | Tuberculinum bovinum- prepared from the pus of tuberculosis abscess. |
| 144 | Tuberculinum Koch- culture of Mycobacterium tuberculosis. |
| 145 | Tuberculinum Marmoreck- from horses vaccinated with Tuberculosis bacilli. |
| 146 | Tuberculinum laricus |
| 147 | Tuberculinum residuum Koch |
| 148 | Bacillinum Burnett- from the sputum of |

| | tuberculosis patients containing the bacteria. |
|---|---|
| 149 | Bacillinum testium- prepared from the testicle of tuberculosis patient. |
| 150 | Diluted B.C.G.- from vaccine B.C. |
| 151 | Actinomyces |
| 152 | Adenoidum |
| 153 | Arteriosclerosis |
| 154 | Bacillus pyocyanaeus |
| 155 | Bilharzia |
| 156 | Brucella melitensis |
| 157 | Cysticercosis |
| 158 | Egg vaccine |
| 159 | Epihysterinum |
| 160 | Framboesinum |
| 161 | Haffkine |
| 162 | Osseinum |
| 163 | Ringworm |

# APPENDIX C. Schedule-calendar for Homeopathic Remedies.

| Day | Date | Remedy, Potency, Notes |
|---|---|---|
| 1 | | |
| 2 | | |
| 3 | | |
| 4 | | |
| 5 | | |
| 6 | | |
| 7 | | |
| 8 | | |
| 9 | | |
| 10 | | |
| 11 | | |
| 12 | | |
| 13 | | |
| 14 | | |
| 15 | | |
| 16 | | |
| 17 | | |
| 18 | | |
| 19 | | |
| 20 | | |
| 21 | | |
| 22 | | |
| 23 | | |
| 24 | | |
| 25 | | |
| 26 | | |
| 27 | | |
| 28 | | |
| 29 | | |
| 30 | | |
| 31 | | |

Example:

| Day | Date | Remedy, Potency, Notes |
|---|---|---|
| 1 | **Oct. 5** | Arnica 30 CH |
| 2 | 6 | --- |
| 3 | 7 | --- |
| 4 | 8 | --- |
| 5 | 9 | --- |
| 6 | 10 | --- |
| 7 | 11 | Silicea 6 CH |
| 8 | 12 | --- |
| 9 | 13 | Silicea 6 CH |
| 10 | 14 | --- |
| 11 | 15 | --- |
| 12 | 16 | |
| 13 | 17 | |
| 14 | 18 | Bryonia 12 CH |
| 15 | 19 | --- |
| 16 | 20 | --- |
| 17 | 21 | --- |
| 18 | 22 | --- |
| 19 | 23 | --- |
| 20 | 24 | --- |
| 21 | 25 | --- |
| 22 | 26 | --- |
| 23 | 27 | --- |
| 24 | 28 | --- |
| 25 | 29 | --- |
| 26 | 30 | --- |
| 27 | 31 | --- |
| 28 | Nov. 1 | Arnica 12 CH |
| 29 | | |
| 30 | | |
| 31 | | |

# APPENDIX D.  Full List of Homeopathic Remedies, Numbered

A  ------------------------

1   A.C.T.H.
2   Abies Canadensis
3   Abies Nigra
4   Abrotanum
5   Absinthium
6   Acacia Arabica
7   Acalypha Indica
8   Acetaldehyde
9   Acetanilidum
10  Aceticum Acidum
11  Acetylsalicylicum Acidum
12  Achyranthis Calea
13  Aconite, or Aconitum Nap
14  Aconitum Ferox
15  Aconitum Lycoctonum
16  Aconitum Napellus
17  Aconitum, Radix
18  Acorus Calamus, or Calamus
19  Actaea Spicata Acrylate
20  Actaea Rac, or Cimicifuga
21  Actaea Spic
22  Adamas
23  Adelheidsquelle Adenosinum
24  Cyclophosphoricum
25  Adeps Suillus
26  Adipose Tissue
27  Adonis Vernalis

28  Adrenal Cortex
29  Adrenal Gland
30  Adrenalinum, or Epinephrine
31  Adrenocorticotrophin
32  Aesculinum
33  Aesculus Carnea, Flos
34  Aesculus Glabra
35  Aesculus Hippocastanum
36  Aesculus Hippocastanum Flos
37  Aethiops Antimonialis Aethiops
38  Mercurialis-Mineralis
39  Aethusa Cynapium
40  Agaricinum
41  Agaricus Campanulatus
42  Agaricus Campestris
43  Agaricus Citrinus
44  Agaricus Emeticus
45  Agaricus Muscarius
46  Agaricus Pantherinus
47  Agaricus Phalloides
48  Agaricus Procerus
49  Agaricus Semiglobatus
50  Agaricus Stercorarius
51  Agave Americana
52  Agave Tequilana
53  Agnus Castus
54  Agraphis Nutans
55  Agrimonia Eupatoria
56  Agrimonia Eupatoria, Flos
57  Agrimonia Odorata, Flos
58  Agrostemma Githago
59  Ailanthus Glandulosus
60  Aletris Farinosa
61  Alfalfa
62  Alisma Plantago
63  Allium Cepa
64  Allium Sativum

65 Alloxanum
66 Alnus Glutinosa
67 Alnus Serrulata
68 Aloe Socotrina
69 Alstonia Constricta
70 Alstonia Scholaris
71 Althaea Officinalis
72 Alumen, or Alum
73 Alumina
74 Alumina Silicata
75 Aluminum Metallicum
76 Aluminum Muriaticum
77 Ambra Grisea
78 Ambrosia Artemisiaefolia
79 Ammi Visnaga
80 Ammoniacum Gummi
81 Ammonium Aceticum
82 Ammonium Benzoicum
83 Ammonium Bromatum
84 Ammonium Carbonicum
85 Ammonium Causticum
86 Ammonium Citricum
87 Ammonium Iodatum
88 Ammonium Muriaticum
89 Ammonium Nitricum
90 Ammonium Phosphoricum
91 Ammonium Picricum
92 Ammonium Tartaricum
93 Ammonium Valerianicum
94 Ammonium Vanadium
95 Amorphophallus Rivieri
96 Ampelopsis Quinquefolia
97 Amygdala Amara
98 Amygdalae Amarae Aqua
99 Amygdalae Amarae Oleum
100 Amygdalus Persica
101 Amyl Nitrosum
102 Anacardium Occidentale

103 Anacardium Orientale
104 Anagallis Arvensis
105 Ananassa
106 Anas Barbariae Hepatis Et Cordis Extractum
107 Anatherum Muricatum
108 Anchusa Officinalis
109 Anemone Nemorosa
110 Anemopsis Californica
111 Anethum Graveolens
112 Angelica Archangelica
113 Angelica Atropurpurea
114 Angelica Sinensis, Radix
115 Angophora Lanceolata
116 Angustura Vera
117 Anhalonium Lewinii
118 Anilinum
119 Anilinum Sulphuricum
120 Anisum
121 Anthemis Nobilis
122 Anthemis Pyrethrum
123 Anthoxanthum Odoratum
124 Anthracinum(anthrax)
125 Antimonium Arsenicicum
126 Antimonium Crudum
127 Antimonium Iodatum
128 Antimonium Muriaticum
129 Antimonium Oxydatum
130 Antimonium Sulphuratum Aureum
131 Antimonium Tartaricum
132 Antipyrinum
133 Apatite
134 Apiolum
135 Apis Mellifica
136 Apis Venenum Purum
137 Apium Graveolens
138 Apocynum Androsaemifolium

139 Apocynum Cannabinum
140 Apomorphinum
141 Apomorphinum Muriaticum
142 Aqua Marina
143 Aquilegia Vulgaris
144 Aralia Hispida
145 Aralia Quinquefolia
146 Aralia Racemosa
147 Aranea Diadema
148 Arbutinum
149 Arbutus Andrachne
150 Areca Catechu
151 Argemone Mexicana
152 Argentum Cyanatum
153 Argentum Iodatum
154 Argentum Metallicum
155 Argentum Muriaticum
156 Argentum Nitricum
157 Argentum Oxydatum
158 Argentum Phosphoricum
159 Aristolochia Clematitis
160 Aristolochia Milhomens
161 Aristolochia Serpentaria
162 Arnica Montana
163 Arnica Montana, Radix
164 Arsenicum Album
165 Arsenicum Bromatum
166 Arsenicum Iodatum
167 Arsenicum Metallicum
168 Arsenicum Sulphuratum Flavum
169 Arsenicum Sulphuratum Rubrum
170 Artemisia Vulgaris
171 Arum Dracontium
172 Arum Italicum
173 Arum Maculatum
174 Arum Triphyllum

175 Arundo Mauritanica
176 Asafoetida
177 Asarum Canadense
178 Asarum Europaeum
179 Asclepias Curassavica
180 Asclepias Incarnata
181 Asclepias Syriaca
182 Asclepias Tuberosa
183 Asclepias Vincetoxicum
184 Asclepias Vincetoxicum Folia
185 Asimina Triloba
186 Asparagus Officinalis
187 Asperula Odorata
188 Astacus Fluviatilis
189 Asterias Rubens
190 Astragalus Menziesii
191 Atropinum
192 Atropinum Sulphuricum
193 Aurum Bromatum
194 Aurum Iodatum
195 Aurum Met
196 Arum Mur
197 Aurum Muriaticum Kalinatum
    Aurum Muriaticum
198 Natronatum
199 Aurum Sulphuratum
200 Avena Sativa
201 Aviaire
202 Azadirachta Indica

B -------------------- ---------

1 Bacillinum of Burnet
2 Badiaga
3 Baja
4 Balsamum Peru
5 Baptisia Tinctoria

6 Barosma Cren
7 Baryta Acetica
8 Baryta Carbonica
9 Baryta Iodata
10 Baryta Muriatica
11 BCG
12 Belladonna
13 Belladonna, Radix
14 Bellis Perennis
15 Benzinum
16 Benzinum Dinitricum
17 Benzoicum Acidum
18 Benzoinum
19 Berberinum
20 Berberis Aquifolium
21 Berberis Vulgaris
22 Berberis Vulgaris, Fructus
23 Beryllium Metallicum
24 Beta Vulgaris
25 Betainum Muriaticum
26 Betula Pendula, Cortex
27 Betula Pendula, Folia
28 Bismuthum Metallicum
29 Bismuthum Oxydatum
30 Bismuthum Subnitricum
31 Bixa Orellana
32 Blatta Americana
33 Blatta Orientalis
34 Boldo
35 Boletus Luridus
36 Boletus Satanas
37 Bombyx Processionea
38 Borago Officinalis
39 Borax
40 Boricum Acidum
41 Botulinum

42 Bovista
43 Brassica Napus
44 Bromelain
45 Bromium
46 Bromus Ramosus, Flos
47 Brucinum
48 Bryonia Alba
49 Bufo Rana
50 Bunias Orientalis
51 Buthus Australis
52 Butyricum Acidum
53 Buxus Sempervirens

**C** --------------------------

1 Cacao
2 Cactus Grandiflorus
3 Cadmium Bromatum
4 Cadmium Iodatum
5 Cadmium Metallicum
6 Cadmium Muriaticum
7 Cadmium Sulphuratum
8 Cadmium Sulphuricum
9 Caffeinum
10 Cahinca
11 Cajuputum
12 Caladium Seguinum
13 Calcarea Acetica
14 Calcarea Arsenicica
15 Calcarea Carbonica
16 Calcarea Caustica
17 Calcarea Fluorica
18 Calcarea Hypochlorata
19 Calcarea Hypophosphorosa
20 Calcarea Iodata

21 Calcarea Lactica
22 Calcarea Muriatica
23 Calcarea Oxalica
24 Calcarea Phosphorica
25 Calcarea Picrata
26 Calcarea Silicata
27 Calcarea Sulphurica
28 Calendula Officinalis
29 Calluna Vulgaris, Flos
30 Calotropis Gigantea
31 Caltha Palustris
32 Camphora
33 Camphora Monobromata
34 Camphoricum Acidum
35 Canchalagua
36 Candida Albicans
37 Candida Parapsilosis
38 Canine Dapp
39 Cantharidinum
40 Cantharis
41 Capsicum, Capsicum Annuum
42 Carbo Animalis
43 Carbo Vegetabilis
44 Carbolicum Acidum
45 Carboneum
46 Carboneum Chloratum
47 Carboneum Hydrogenisatum
48 Carboneum Oxygenisatum
49 Carboneum Sulphuratum
50 Carcinosinum
51 Cardiospermum
52 Carduus Benedictus
53 Carduus Marianus
54 Carpinus Betulus, Flos
55 Cartilago Suis

56 Carum Carvi
57 Cascarilla
58 Cassada
59 Castanea Sativa, Flos
60 Castanea Vesca
61 Castor Equi
62 Castoreum
63 Catalpa Bignonioides
64 Caulophyllum Thalictroides
65 Causticum
66 Ceanothus Americanus
67 Cedron
68 Celtis Occidentalis
69 Cenchris Contortrix
70 Centaurea Tagana
71 Centaurium Umbellatum, Flos
72 Cephalanthus Occidentalis
73 Cerasus Virginiana
74 Ceratostigma Willmottianum, Flos
75 Cereus Bonplandii
76 Cereus Serpentinus
77 Cerium Oxalicum
78 Cetraria Islandica
79 Chamomilla
80 Cheiranthus Cheiri
81 Chelidonium Majus
82 Chelidonium Majus, Radix
83 Chelone Glabra
84 Chenopodii Glauci Aphis
85 Chenopodium Anthelminticum
86 Chenopodium Vulvaria
87 Chimaphila Maculata
88 Chimaphila Umbellata
89 Chininum Arsenicicum
90 Chininum Arsenicosum

91  Chininum Muriaticum
92  Chininum Purum
93  Chininum Salicylicum
94  Chininum Sulphuricum
95  Chionanthus Virginica
96  Chloralum
97  Chloramphenicolum
98  Chlorinum
99  Chloroforum
100 Chlorpromazinum
101 Cholera
102 Cholesterinum
103 Cholinum
104 Chromicum Acidum
105 Chromium Kali Sulphuricum
106 Chromium Oxydatum
107 Chromium Sulphuricum
108 Chrysanthemum Leucanthemum
109 Chrysarobinum
110 Cicer Arietinum
111 Cichorium Intybus
112 Cichorium Intybus, Flos
113 Cicuta Maculata
114 Cicuta Virosa
115 Cimex Lectularius
116 Cimicifuga Racemosa
117 Cina
118 Cinchona Officinalis
119 Cinchonium Sulphuricum
120 Cineraria Maritima
121 Cineraria Maritima,Succus
122 Cinnamomum
123 Cistus Canadensis
124 Citricum Acidum
125 Citrus Decumana

126 Citrus Limonum
127 Citrus Vulgaris
128 Clematis Erecta
129 Clematis Virginiana
130 Clematis Vitalba, Flos
131 Clematis Vitalba, Folia
132 Cobaltum Metallicum
133 Cobaltum Muriaticum
134 Cobaltum Nitricum
135 Coccinella Septempunctata
136 Cocculus Indicus
137 Coccus Cacti
138 Cochlearia Armoracia
139 Cochlearia Officinalis
140 Coenzyme A
141 Coffea Cruda
142 Coffea Tosta
143 Colchicinum
144 Colchicum Autumnale
145 Colibacillinum
146 Collinsonia Canadensis
147 Colocynthinum
148 Colocynthis
149 Colostrum
150 Comocladia Dentata
151 Conchiolinum
152 Condurango
153 Coniinum
154 Coniinum Bromatum
155 Conium Maculatum
156 Convallaria Majalis
157 Convolvulus Arvensis
158 Copaiva Officinalis
159 Corallium Rubrum
160 Corallorhiza Odontorhiza

161 Coriaria Ruscifolia
162 Cornus Alternifolia
163 Cornus Circinata
164 Cornus Florida
165 Cortisone Aceticum
166 Corydalis Canadensis
167 Cotyledon Umbilicus
168 Coumarinum
169 Crataegus Oxyacantha
170 Cresolum
171 Crocus Sativus
172 Crotalus Cascavella
173 Crotalus Horridus
174 Croton Tiglium
175 Crotonchloralum
176 Cubeba Officinalis
177 Cucurbita Citrullus
178 Cucurbita Pepo. Flos
179 Cucurbita Pepo, Semen
180 Culex Musca
181 Cuphea Petiolata
182 Cupressus Australis
183 Cupressus Lawsoniana
184 Cuprum Aceticum
185 Cuprum Ammonio-Sulphuricum
186 Cuprum Arsenicosum
187 Cuprum Carbonicum
188 Cuprum Metallicum
189 Cuprum Muriaticum
190 Cuprum Nitricum
191 Cuprum Oxydatum Nigrum
192 Cuprum Sulphuricum
193 Curare
194 Cyclamen Europaeum
195 Cydonia Vulgaris

196 Cynara Scolymus
197 Cynodon Dactylon
198 Cypripedium Pubescens
199 Cysteinum
200 Cytisus Scoparius

**D** -------------------------

1 Damiana
2 Daphne Indica
3 Datura Arborea
4 Datura Metel
5 DDT
6 Delphininum
7 Derris Pinnata
8 Dichapetalum
9 Dictamnus Albus
10 Digitalinum
11 Digitalis Purpurea
12 Digitoxinum
13 Dioscorea Villosa
14 Dioscoreinum
15 Diphtherinum
16 Diphtherotozinum
17 Diptherinum
18 Diptherotoxinum
19 Dirca Palustris
20 DNA
21 Dolichos Pruriens
22 Doryphora Decemlineata
23 Draba Verna
24 Drosera Rotundifolia
25 DTTAB(Diptheria)
26 Duboisia Myoporoides

27  Dulcamara
28  Dulcamara, Flos
29  Dysentery

# E ---------------------------

1  E. Coli
2  Ear, Labyrinth of (inner ear)
3  Ear, Middle
4  Eberthinum
5  Echinacea Angustifolia
6  Echinacea Purpurea
7  Elaeis Guineensis
8  Elaps Corallinus
9  Elaterium
10  Embryo Suis
11  Emetinum
12  Enterotoccinum
13  Eosinum Natrum
14  Ephedra Vulgaris
15  Epigaea Repens
16  Epilobium Palustre
17  Epiphegus Virginiana
18  Equisetum Arvense
19  Equisetum Hyemale
20  Eranthis Hyemalis
21  Erechtites Hieracifolia
22  Erigeron Canadensis
23  Eriodictyon Californicum
24  Erodium
25  Eryngium Aquaticum
26  Eryngium Maritimum
27  Erythraea Centaurium
28  Eschscholtzia Californica

29 Eserinum
30 Etherum
31 Ethylicum
32 Ethylum Nitricum
33 Eucalyptol
34 Eucalyptus Globulus
35 Eugenia Caryophyllata
36 Eugenia Jambosa
37 Euonymus Atropurpureus
38 Euonymus Europaeus
39 Eupatorium Aromaticum
40 Eupatorium Cannabinum
41 Eupatorium Perfoliatum
42 Eupatorium Purpureum
43 Euphorbia Amygdaloides
44 Euphorbia Corollata
45 Euphorbia Cyparissias
46 Euphorbia Hypericifolia
47 Euphorbia Lathyris
48 Euphorbia Pilulifera
49 Euphorbium Officinarum
50 Euphrasia Officinalis
51 Eupion
52 Eyebright herb

F --------------------------

1 Fagopyrum Esculentum
2 Fagus Sylvatica
3 Fagus Sylvatica, Flos
4 Fel Tauri
5 Ferrum Aceticum
6 Ferrum Arsenicicum
7 Ferrum Bromatum

8 Ferrum Carbonicum
9 Ferrum Citricum
10 Ferrum Cyanatum
11 Ferrum Iodatum
12 Ferrum Lacticum
13 Ferrum Metallicum
14 Ferrum Muriaticum
15 Ferrum Pernitricum
16 Ferrum Phosphoricum
17 Ferrum Picricum
18 Ferrum Sulphuricum
19 Ferrum Tartaricum
20 Ferula Glauca
21 Ficus Religiosa
22 Filix Mas
23 Foeniculum Vulgare
24 Folliculinum
25 Formalinum
26 Formica Rufa
27 Formicum Acidum
28 Fragaria Vesca
29 Franciscea Uniflora
30 Fraxinus Americana
31 Fraxinus Excelsior
32 Fuchsinum
33 Fucus Vesiculosus
34 Fumaria Officinalis
35 Fumaricum Acidum
36 Funiculus Umbilicalis Suis

G --------------------------

1 Galanthus Nivalis

2 Galega Officinalis
3 Galium Aparine
4 Gallicum Acidum
5 Galphimia Glauca
6 Gambogia
7 Garlic
8 Gaultheria Procumbens
9 Gelsemium Sempervirens
10 Genista Tinctoria
11 Gentiana Cruciata
12 Gentiana Lutea
13 Gentiana Quinqueflora
14 Gentianella Amarella, Flos
15 Geranium Maculatum
16 Geranium Robertianum
17 Geum Rivale
18 Geum Urbanum
19 Ginkgo Biloba
20 Glandula Suprarenalis Suis
21 Glechoma Hederacea
22 Glonoinum
23 Glycerinum
24 Glycogenum
25 Glycyrrhiza Glabra
26 Gnaphalium Leontopodium
27 Gnaphalium Polycephalum
28 Gnaphalium Uliginosum
29 Gonotoxinum
30 Gossypium Herbaccum
31 Granatum
32 Graphites
33 Gratiola Officinalis
34 Grindelia
35 Guaco
36 Guaiacum

37  Guarea Trichilioides
38  Guatteria Gaumeri
39  Gunpowder
40  Gymnocladus Canadensis

**H** --------------------------

1   Haematoxylon Campechianum
2   Haemophilus Infl. B
3   Hair Bulb, Pilo Sebaceous Zone
4   HamamelisVirginiana
5   Haronga Madagas-cariensis
6   Hedeoma Pulegioides
7   Hedera Helix
8   Hekla Lava
9   Helianthemum Nummularium, Flos
10  Helianthus Annuus
11  Heliotropium Peruvianum
12  Helix Tosta
13  Helleborus Foetidus
14  Helleborus Niger
15  Helleborus Viridis
16  Heloderma
17  Helonias Dioica
18  Hepar Suis
19  Hepar Sulphuris Calcareum
20  Hepar Sulphuris Kalinum
21  Hepatica Triloba
22  Hepatitis A
23  Hepatitis B
24  Hepatitis C
25  Heracleum Sphondylium
26  Herpes Zoster
27  Hippozaeninum

28  Hippuricum Acidum
29  Hirudinum
30  Histaminum Hydrochloricum
31  Hoang-Nan
32  Hoitzia Coccinea
33  Holarrhena Antidysenterica
34  Homarus
35  Hottonia Palustris, Flos
36  Humulus Lupulus
37  Hura Brasiliensis
38  Hura Crepitans
39  Hydrangea Arborescens
40  Hydrastininum Muriaticum
41  Hydrastis Canadensis
42  Hydrocotyle Asiatica
43  Hydrocyanicum Acidum
44  Hydrofluoricum Acidum
45  Hydrophis Cyanocinctus
46  Hydrophyllum Virginianum
47  Hyoscyaminum
48  Hyoscyaminum
49  Hydrobromatum
50  Hyoscyamus Niger
51  Hypericum Perforatum
52  Hypothalamus

I ---------------------------

1  Iberis Amara
2  Ichthyolum
3  Ignatia Amara
4  Ilex Aquifolium
5  Ilex Aquifolium, Flos
6  Ilex Paraguariensis

7   Illicium Anisatum
8   Impatiens Glandulifera, Flos
9   Imperatoria Ostruthium
10  Indigo
11  Indium Metallicum
12  Indolum
13  Influenzinum
14  Inula Helenium
15  Iodium
16  Iodoformum
17  Ipecacuanha
18  Ipomoea Stans
19  Iridium Metallicum
20  Iris Florentina
21  Iris Foetidissima
22  Iris Germanica
23  Iris Tenax
24  Iris Versicolor

J -------------------------

1   Jacaranda Caroba
2   Jalapa
3   Jasminum Officinale
4   Jasper
5   Jatropha Curcas
6   Jatropha Urens
7   Jequirity
8   Jonesia Asoca
9   Juglans Cinerea
10  Juglans Regia
11  Juglans Regia, Flos
12  Juncus Effusus
13  Juniperus Communis

14  Juniperus Virginiana
15  Justicia Adhatoda

# K ------------------------

1   Kali Aceticum
2   Kali Arsenicosum
3   Kali Bichromicum
4   Kali Bromatum
5   Kali Carbonicum
6   Kali Causticum
7   Kali Chloricum
8   Kali Chromicum
9   Kali Cyanatum
10  Kali Ferrocyanatum
11  Kali Iodatum
12  Kali Muriaticum
13  Kali Nitricum
14  Kali Oxalicum
15  Kali Permanganicum
16  Kali Phosphoricum
17  Kali Picricum
18  Kali Silicatum
19  Kali Sulphuricum
20  Kali Tartaricum
21  Kali Telluricum
22  Kalmia Latifolia
23  Kamala
24  Karaka
25  Karwinskia Humboldtiana
26  Kino Australiensis
27  Kousso
28  Kreosotum

**L** ------------------------

1. Laburnum Anagyroides
2. Lac Caninum
3. Lac Defloratum
4. Lac Felinum
5. Lac Maternum
6. Lac Vaccinum
7. Lacerta Agilis
8. Lachesis Mutus
9. Lachnanthes Tinctoria
10. Lacticum Acidum
11. Lactuca Virosa
12. Lamium Album
13. Lapis Albus
14. Lappa Major
15. Larix Decidua, Flos
16. Lathyrus Cicera
17. Lathyrus Sativus
18. Latrodectus Katipo
19. Latrodectus Mactans
20. Laurocerasus
21. Lecithin granules
22. Lecithin potenized
23. Ledum Palustre
24. Lemna Minor
25. Leonurus Cardiaca
26. Lepidium Bonariense
27. Leptandra Virginica
28. Lespedeza Capitata
29. Levico
30. Levisticum Officinale
31. Levomepromazinum
32. Liatris Spicata
33. Lilium Tigrinum

34  Limulus
35  Linaria Vulgaris
36  Linum Catharticum
37  Linum Usitatissimum
38  Lithium Benzoicum
39  Lithium Bromatum
40  Lithium Carbonicum
41  Lithium Muriaticum
42  Lobelia Cardinalis
43  Lobelia Erinus
44  Lobelia Inflata
45  Lobelia Purpurescens
46  Lobelia Syphilitica
47  Lobelinum
48  Lolium Temulentum
49  Lonicera Caprifolium, Flos
50  Lonicera Periclymenum
51  Lonicera Xylosteum
52  Lophophytum Leandri
53  Luesinum
54  Luffa Operculata
55  Lupulinum
56  Lycopersicum Esculentum
57  Lycopodium Clavatum
58  Lycopus Virginicus
59  Lysimachia Nummularia
60  Lyssin
61  Lyssinum

M  --------------------------

1  Macrotinum
2  Magnesia Carbonica
3  Magnesia Muriatica

.

4   Magnesia Oxydata
5   Magnesia Phosphorica
6   Magnesia Sulphurica
7   Magnesium Metallicum
8   Magnolia Glauca
9   Magnolia Grandiflora
10  Malaria Off.
11  Malus Pumila, Flos
12  Mancinella
13  Mandragora Officinarum
14  Manganum Aceticum
15  Manganum Carbonicum
16  Manganum Metallicum
17  Manganum Muriaticum
18  Manganum Oxydatum Nativum
19  Manganum Oxydatum Nigrum
20  Manganum Phosphoricum
21  Manganum Sulphuricum
22  Mangifera Indica
23  Marrubium Vulgare
24  Matico
25  Matthiola Graeca
26  Medorrhinum(Gonorrheal virus)
27  Medulla Ossis Suis
28  Medusa
29  Melastoma Ackermani
30  Melilotus Alba
31  Melilotus Officinalis
32  Melissa Officinalis
33  Menispermum Canadense
34  Mentha Piperita
35  Mentha Pulegium
36  Mentha Viridis
37  Mentholum
38  Menyanthes Trifoliata

| | |
|---|---|
| 39 | Mephitis Mephitica |
| 40 | Mercurialis Perennis |
| 41 | Mercurius Aceticus |
| 42 | Mercurius Auratus |
| 43 | Mercurius Bromatus |
| 44 | Mercurius Corrosivus |
| 45 | Mercurius Cum Kali Iodatus |
| 46 | Mercurius Cyanatus |
| 47 | Mercurius Dulcis |
| 48 | Mercurius Iodatus Flavus |
| 49 | Mercurius Iodatus Ruber |
| 50 | Mercurius Methylenus |
| 51 | Mercurius Nitricus |
| 52 | Mercurius Praecipitatus Albus |
| 53 | Mercurius Praecipitatus Ruber |
| 54 | Mercurius Solubilis |
| 55 | Mercurius Sulphocyanatus |
| 56 | Mercurius Sulphuratus Ruber |
| 57 | Mercurius Sulphuricus |
| 58 | Mercurius Vivus |
| 59 | Methylene Blue |
| 60 | Mezereum |
| 61 | Millefolium |
| 62 | Mimosa Pudica |
| 63 | Mimulus Guttatus, Flos |
| 64 | Mitchella Repens |
| 65 | Momordica Balsamina |
| 66 | Mononucleosis |
| 67 | Monotropa Uniflora |
| 68 | Morbillinum(Measles) |
| 69 | Moschus |
| 70 | Mucosa Nasalis Suis |
| 71 | Mullein Essence |
| 72 | Murex Purpurea |
| 73 | Muriaticum Acidum |

74 Musa Sapientum
75 Mygale
76 Myosotis Arvensis
77 Myrica Cerifera
78 Myristica Sebifera
79 Myrrha
80 Myrtus Communis

**N** ------------------------

1 Nabalus Serpentarius
2 Nadidum
3 Naja Tripudians
4 Naphthalinum
5 Narceinum
6 Narcissus, Pseudo-
7 Narcissus
8 Narcotinum
9 Nasturtium Aquaticum
10 Natrum Arsenicicum
11 Natrum Bicarbonicum
12 Natrum Bromatum
13 Natrum Carbonicum
14 Natrum Fluoratum
15 Natrum Hypochlorosum
16 Natrum Lacticum
17 Natrum Muriaticum
18 Natrum Nitricum
19 Natrum Nitrosum
20 Natrum Oxalaceticum
21 Natrum Phosphoricum
22 Natrum Pyruvicum
23 Natrum Salicylicum
24 Natrum Silicofluoricum

25 Natrum Sulphuratum
26 Natrum Sulphuricum
27 Natrum Sulphurosum
28 Negundo
29 Nepenthes
30 Nepeta Cataria
31 Niccolum Carbonicum
32 Niccolum Metallicum
33 Niccolum Sulphuricum
34 Nicotinamidum
35 Nicotinum
36 Nitri Spiritus Dulcis
37 Nitricum Acidum
38 Nitrogenum Oxygenatum
39 Nitromuriaticum Acidum
40 Nosode Kit
41 Nosode-Select your own
42 Nuclear Radiation
43 Nuphar Luteum
44 Nux Moschata
45 Nux Vomica
46 Nymphaea Odorata

**O** --------------------------

1 Ocimum Basilicum
2 Ocimum Canum
3 Ocimum Sanctum
4 Oenanthe Crocata
5 Oenothera Biennis
6 Olea Europaea, Flos
7 Oleander
8 Oleum Animale

9   Oleum Carvi
10  Oleum Morrhuae
11  Oleum Ricini
12  Oleum Santali
13  Olibanum
14  Oniscus
15  Ononis Spinosa
16  Onopordum
17  Onosmodium Virginianum
18  Oophorinum
19  Opuntia Vulgaris
20  Orchitinum
21  Oreodaphne Californica
22  Origanum Majorana
23  Ornithogalum Umbellatum
24  Ornithogalum Umbellatum, Flos
25  Oroticum Acidum
26  Oscillococcinum
27  Osmium Metallicum
28  Ostrya
29  Ova Tosta
30  Ovi Gallinae Pellicula
31  Oxalicum Acidum
32  Oxalis Acetosella
33  Oxydendrum Arboreum
34  Oxytropis Lambertii

P ------------------------

1   Paeonia Officinalis
2   Palladium Metallicum

3   Paloondo
4   Pancreas Suis
5   Pancreatinum
6   Paraffinum
7   Parathormonum
8   Parathyroid
9   Paratyphoidinum B
10  Pareira Brava
11  Parietaria Officinalis
12  Paris Quadrifolia
13  Paronichia Illecebrum
14  Parotidinum(Mumps)
15  Parthenium
16  Passiflora Incarnata
17  Pastinaca Sativa
18  Paullinia Pinnata
19  Paullinia Sorbilis
20  Pecten
21  Pediculus Capitis
22  Penicillinum
23  Penthorum Sedoides
24  Pepsinum
25  Perhexilinum
26  Persea Americana
27  Pertussinum(Whooping Cough)
28  Petiveria Tetrandra
29  Petroleum
30  Petroselinum Sativum
31  Phallus Impudicus
32  Phaseolus
33  Phellandrium Aquaticum
34  Phenacetinum
35  Phenobarbitalum

36 Phloridzinum
37 Phosphoricum Acidum
38 Phosphorus
39 Physalis Alkekenge
40 Physotigma Venenosum
41 Phytolacca Decandra
42 Pichi
43 Picricum Acidum
44 Picrotoxinum
45 Pilocarpinum
46 Pilocarpinum Muriaticum
47 Pilocarpinum Nitricum
48 Pilocarpus
49 Pimenta Officinalis
50 Pimpinella Saxifraga
51 Pinus Lambertiana
52 Pinus Sylvestris
53 Pinus Sylvestris, Flos
54 Piper Methysticum
55 Piper Nigrum
56 Piperazinum
57 Piscidia Erythrina
58 Pituitarum Posterium
59 Pix Liquida
60 Placenta Totalis Suis
61 Plague
62 Plantago Major
63 Platanus
64 Platinum Metallicum
65 Platinum Muriaticum
66 Plectranthus Fruticosus
67 Plumbago Littoralis
68 Plumbum Aceticum

69 Plumbum Carbonicum
70 Plumbum Chromicum
71 Plumbum Iodatum
72 Plumbum Metallicum
73 Pneumococcinum
74 Podophyllinum
75 Podophyllum Peltatum
76 Polio
77 Polygonum Punctatum
78 Polygonum Sagittatum
79 Polyporus Officinalis
80 Polyporus Pinicola
81 Populus Candicans
82 Populus Tremula, Flos
83 Populus Tremuloides
84 Potentilla Anserina
85 Pothos Foetidus
86 Primula Obconica
87 Primula Veris
88 Primula Vulgaris
89 Proteus Bulgaris
90 Proteus Vulgaris
91 Prunus Cerasifera, Flos
92 Prunus Padus
93 Prunus Spinosa
94 Prunus Virginiana
95 Psorinum
96 Ptelea Trifoliata
97 Pulex Irritans
98 Pulsatilla Niger
99 Pulsatilla Nuttalliana
100 Pyrethrum Parthenium
101 Pyridoxinum Hydrochloricum

102  Pyrogenium-sepsis
103  Pyrus Americana

**Q** ------------------------

1. Quassia Amara
2. Quebracho
3. Quercus Glandium Spiritus
4. Quercus Robur
5. Quercus Robur, Flos
6. Quillaja Saponaria

**R** ------------------------

1. Radium Bromatum
2. Ranunculus Acris
3. Ranunculus Bulbosus
4. Ranunculus Ficaria
5. Ranunculus Glacialis
6. Ranunculus Repens
7. Ranunculus Sceleratus
8. Raphanus Sativus
9. Ratanhia
10. Rauwolfia Serpentina
11. Reserpinum
12. Resina Laricis
13. Resorcinum
14. Rhamnus Californica
15. Rhamnus Cathartica
16. Rhamnus Frangula
17. Rhamnus Purshiana
18. Rheum Officinale

19. Rhodium Metallicum
20. Rhododendron Chrysanthum
21. Rhus Aromatica
22. Rhus Diversiloba
23. Rhus Glabra
24. Rhus Toxicodendron
25. Rhus Venenata
26. Riboflavinum
27. Ricinus Communis
28. RNA
29. Robinia Pseudoacacia
30. Rock Water
31. Rosa Canina
32. Rosa Canina, Flos
33. Rosa Damascena
34. Rosmarinus Officinalis
35. Rubella(German Measles)
36. Rubeola(Measles)
37. Rubia Tinctorum
38. Rumex Acetosa
39. Rumex Crispus
40. Rumex Obtusifolius
41. Russula Foetens
42. Ruta Graveolens

S --------------------------

1. Sabidilla
2. Sabal Serrulata
3. Sabina
4. Saccharinum
5. Saccharum Lactis
6. Saccharum Officinale

7 Salicinum
8 Salicylicum Acidum
9 Salix Alba
10 Salix Nigra
11 Salix Purpurea
12 Salix Vitellina, Flos
13 Salmonella
14 Salol
15 Salvia Officinalis
16 Samarskite
17 Sambucus Canadensis
18 Sambucus Nigra
19 Sanguinaria Canadensis
20 Sanguinarinum Nitricum
21 Sanicula
22 Santoninum
23 Saponaria Officinalis
24 Saponinum
25 Sarcode-Select your own organ remedy
26 Sarcolacticum Acidum
27 Sarracenia Purpurea
28 Sarsaparilla
29 Sassafras Officinale
30 Scammonium
31 Scarlatinum
32 Secale-Ergot Schinus Molle
33 Scilla Maritima
34 Scleranthus Annuus, Flos
35 Scolopendra
36 Scolopendrium Vulgare
37 Scopolaminum Hydrobromidum
38 Scrophularia Nodosa
39 Scutellaria Lateriflora

40 Secale Cornutum
41 Secale -Ergot
42 Sedum Acre
43 Selenium Metallicum
44 Sempervivum Tectorum
45 Senecio Aureus
46 Senecio Jacobaea
47 Senega Officinalis
48 Senna
49 Sepia
50 Serum Anguillae
51 Serum Anticolibacillaire
52 Serum De Yersin
53 Serum Equi
54 Shigella
55 Silica Marina
56 Silicea
57 Silphium Laciniatum
58 Sinapis Alba
59 Sinapis Arvensis, Flos
60 Sinapis Nigra
61 Sinusitisinum
62 Sium Latifolium
63 Skatolum
64 Skookum Chuck
65 Slag
66 Solaninum
67 Solanum Arrebenta
68 Solanum Carolinense
69 Solanum Mammosum
70 Solanum Nigrum
71 Solanum Oleraceum
72 Solanum Tuberosum

| | |
|---|---|
| 73 | Solidago Virgaurea |
| 74 | Sparteinum Sulphuricum |
| 75 | Spigelia Anthelmia |
| 76 | Spigelia Marilandica |
| 77 | Spilanthes Oleracea |
| 78 | Spinacia |
| 79 | Spiraea Ulmaria |
| 80 | Spiranthes Autumnalis |
| 81 | Spongia Encephalitis |
| 82 | Spongia Tosta |
| 83 | Stachys Betonica |
| 84 | Stannum Iodatum |
| 85 | Stannum Metallicum |
| 86 | Staphyloccoccus Aureus |
| 87 | Staphylococcinum |
| 88 | Staphylotoxinum |
| 89 | Staphysagria |
| 90 | Stellaria Media |
| 91 | Sterculia Acuminata |
| 92 | Stibium Metallicum |
| 93 | Sticta Pulmonaria |
| 94 | Stigmata Maidis |
| 95 | Stillingia Sylvatica |
| 96 | Stramonium |
| 97 | Streptococcinum |
| 98 | Strontium Bromatum |
| 99 | Strontium Carbonicum |
| 100 | Strontium Nitricum |
| 101 | Strophanthus Hispidus |
| 102 | Strophanthus Sarmentosus |
| 103 | Strychninum |
| 104 | Strychinum Arsenicicum |
| 105 | Strychinum Nitricum |

106 Strychninum Phosphoricum
107 Strychninum Sulphuricum
108 Succinicum Acidum
109 Succinum
110 Sulphanilamidum
111 Sulphonalum
112 Sulphur
113 Sulphur Hydrogenisatum
114 Sulphur Iodatum
115 Sulphuricum Acidum
116 Sulphurosum Acidum
117 Sumbul
118 Symphoricarpus Racemosus
119 Symphytum Officinale
120 Syphilinum(Luesinum)
121 Syzygium Jambolanum

T -------------------------

1 Tabacum
2 Tamus Communis
3 Tanacetum Vulgare
4 Tanghinia Venenifera
5 Tannicum Acidum
6 Taraxacum Officinale
7 Taraxacum Officinale, Radix
8 Tarentula Cubensis
9 Tarentula Hispana
10 Tartaricum Acidum
11 Taxus Baccata
12 Tellurium Metallicum
13 Teplitz
14 Terebinthina

15  Tetanotoxinum
16  Tetradymite
17  Teucrium Marum
18  Teucrium Scorodonia
19  Thallium Metallicum
20  Thaspium Aureum
21  Thea Sinensis
22  Theobrominum
23  Theridion
24  Thiaminum Hydrochloricum
25  Thioproperazinum
26  Thiosinaminum
27  Thlaspi Bursa-Pastoris
28  Thuja Lobbi
29  Thuja Occidentalis
30  Thymolum
31  Thymus Serpyllum
32  Thyroidinum
33  Tilia Europaea
34  Titanium Metallicum
35  Tongo
36  Tormentilla
37  Torula Cerevisiae
38  Toxicophis Pugnax
39  Tradescantia Diuretica
40  Tribulus Terrestris
41  Trifolium Pratense
42  Trifolium Repens
43  Trillium Pendulum
44  Trimethylaminum
45  Triosteum Perfoliatum
46  Triticum Repens
47  Tropaeolum Majus

48 Tuberculinum
49 Tuberculinum Residuum
50 Tussilago Farfara
51 Tussilago Fragrans
52 Tussilago Petasites
53 Typhoidinum

**U** ------------------------

1 Ulex Europaeus, Flos
2 Ulmus Fulva
3 Ulmus Procera, Flos
4 Upas Tieute
5 Uranium Nitricum
6 Urea
7 Uricum Acidum
8 Urtica Crenulata
9 Urtica Dioica
10 Urtica Urens
11 Usnea Barbata
12 Ustilago Maidis
13 Uva-Ursi herb
14 Uva-Ursi

**V** ------------------------

1 V.A.B. -BCG
2 Vaccinium Myrtillus
3 Vaccinotoxinum
4 Valeriana Officinalis
5 Vanadium Metallicum
  Varicella enus
6 Mercenaria(Chicken Pox)

7 Variolinum(Smallpox)
8 Veratrinum
9 Veratrum Album
10 Veratrum Nigrum
11 Veratrum Viride
12 Verbascum Thapsus
13 Verbena Hastata
14 Verbena Officinalis
15 Verbena Officinalis, Flos
16 Veronica Beccabunga
17 Veronica Officinalis
18 Vesicaria
19 Vespa Crabro
20 Viburnum Opulus
21 Viburnum Prunifolium
22 Vinca Minor
23 Viloa Odorata
24 Viola Tricolor
25 Vipera Berus
26 Viscum Album
27 Vitamin B12
28 Vitamin K
29 Vitis Vinifera, Flos

**W** ------------------------

1 Wiesbaden
2 Wyethia Helenioides

**X** ------------------------

1 X-Ray

2 Xanthoxylum Fraxineum
3 Xerophyllum Asphodeloides

**Y** -------------------------

1 Yohimbinum
2 Yucca Filamentosa

**Z** -------------------------

1 Zincum Aceticum
2 Zincum Bromatum
3 Zincum Carbonicum
4 Zincum Cyanatum
5 Zincum Gluconicum
6 Zincum Iodatum
7 Zincum Metallicum
8 Zincum Muriaticum
9 Zincum Oxydatum
10 Zincum Phosphoratum
11 Zincum Picricum
12 Zincum Sulphuricum
13 Zincum Valerianicum
14 Zingiber Officinale

# APPENDIX E. Pendulum Charts

The following charts are provided in this Attachment:

CHART B1.  Starting Point and Introductory Questions
CHART B1.  Starting Point and Introductory Questions
CHART A1.  Yes-No-Maybe and Probabilities
CHART A2.  Digits 1 – 9 and Decimal Point
CHART A3.  Letters
CHART S1.  Problems with Answers
CHART A4.  Simple Yes-No
CHART "0 to 10"
CHART "0 to 100"
CHART "0 to 1000"
CHART C1.  What Needs Attention
CHART C1a.  Main Areas of Life
CHART C1b.  Chakras
CHART C2.  Severity of a Condition or Situation
CHART C3.  General Issues
CHART C4.  Body Systems
CHART C5.  Categories of Bach Flower Remedies
CHART C6.  Selecting Potencies of Homeopathic Remedies
CHART C7.  Number of Days to the Next Remedy

# CHART B1 STARTING POINT
## Introductory Questions

QUESTION #1: ..........................

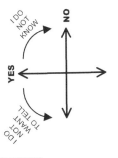

● Please confirm that:
  * I may ask the question as written, or carry out the action as written and
  * You are willing to answer it correctly, and that
  * The answer or the action will be beneficial to me and my family and not harmful to others.

● Please confirm that:
  * There is no negative entity connected to my pendulum or any entity that does not love The Holy Spirit and that
  * There will be no interference from any negative entities in the pendulum reading

● Question: Does my subconscious mind have believes which are not beneficial to me or to my family?

● Question: is the answer going to mislead me into an action or a belief into a positive outcome, while the final outcome will not be beneficial to me or to my family?

● Question: Was the last answer correct?
*(Number the questions so you could ask again, to double check, if some important questions from the session were answered correctly).*

## CHART B1. Starting Point and Introductory Questions

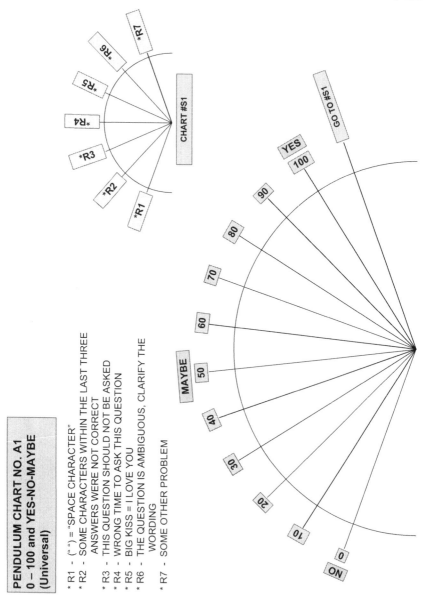

CHART A1. Yes-No-Maybe and Probabilities

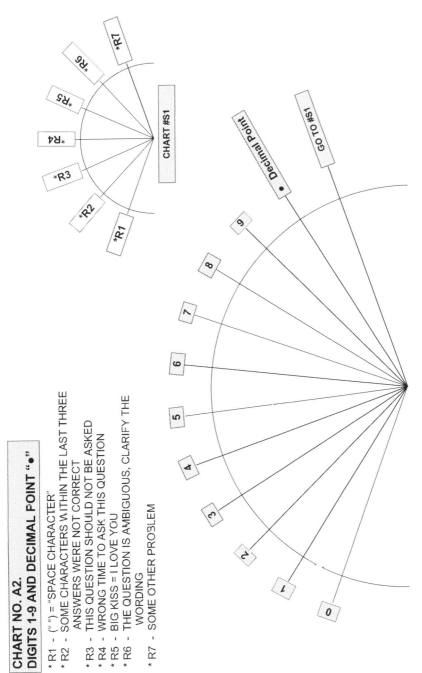

**CHART A2.  Digits 1 – 9 and Decimal Point**

**114**

**CHART NO. A3
LETTERS**

* R1 - (" ") = "SPACE CHARACTER"
* R2 - SOME CHARACTERS WITHIN THE LAST THREE ANSWERS WERE NOT CORRECT
* R3 - THIS QUESTION SHOULD NOT BE ASKED
* R4 - WRONG TIME TO ASK THIS QUESTION
* R5 - BIG KISS = I LOVE YOU
* R6 - THE QUESTION IS AMBIGUOUS, CLARIFY THE WORDING
* R7 - SOME OTHER PROBLEM

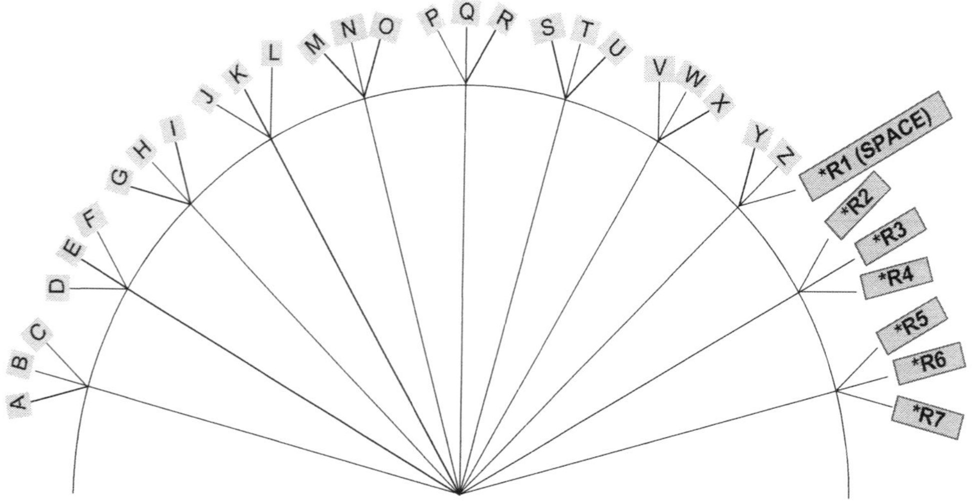

**CHART A3. Letters**

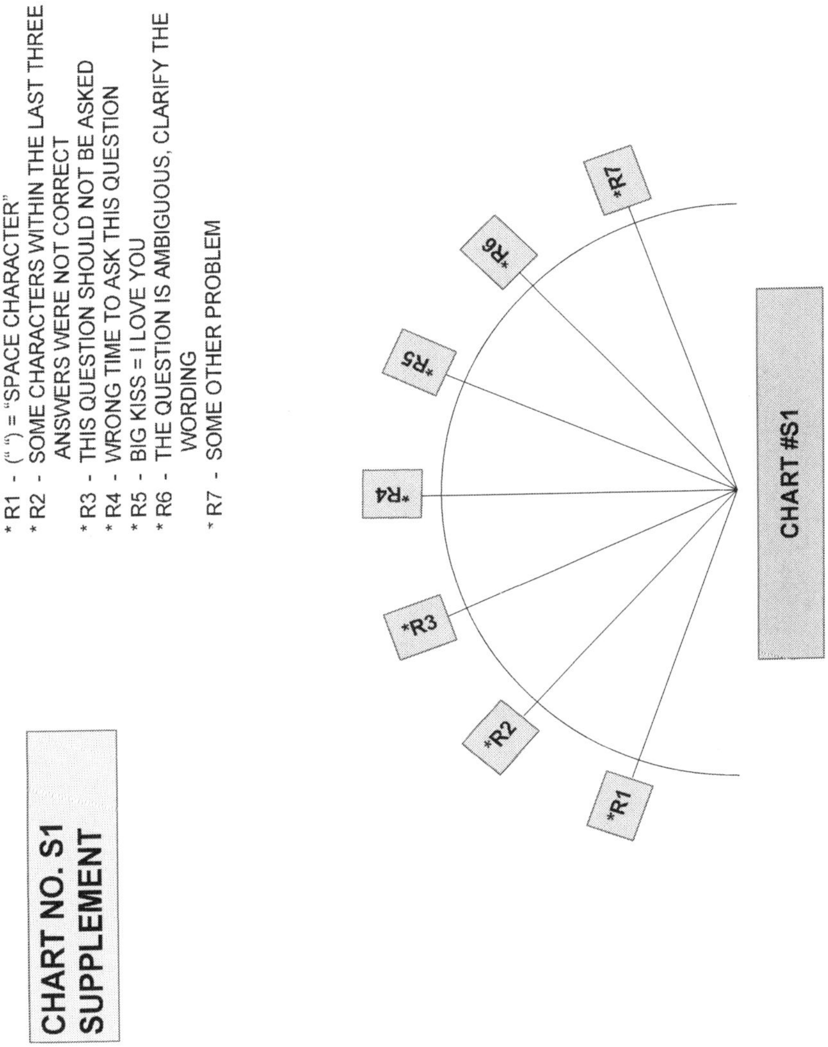
CHART NO. S1
SUPPLEMENT
* R1 - (" ") = "SPACE CHARACTER"
* R2 - SOME CHARACTERS WITHIN THE LAST THREE ANSWERS WERE NOT CORRECT
* R3 - THIS QUESTION SHOULD NOT BE ASKED
* R4 - WRONG TIME TO ASK THIS QUESTION
* R5 - BIG KISS = I LOVE YOU
* R6 - THE QUESTION IS AMBIGUOUS, CLARIFY THE WORDING
* R7 - SOME OTHER PROBLEM
*R1
*R2
*R3
*R4
*R5
*R6
*R7
CHART #S1

***CHART S1. Problems with the Answers***

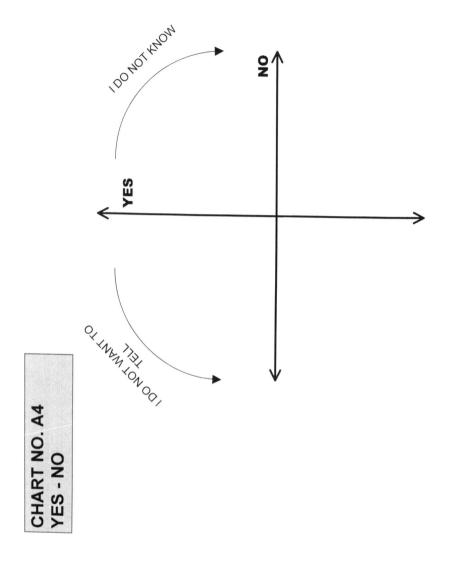

**CHART A4. Simple Yes-No**

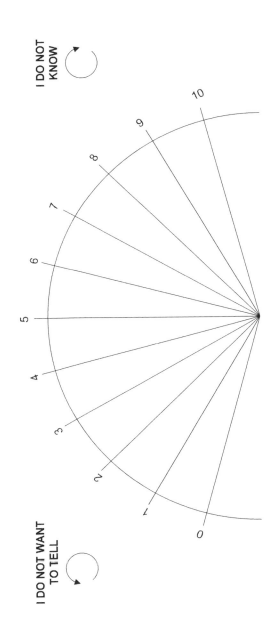

CHART "0 to 10"

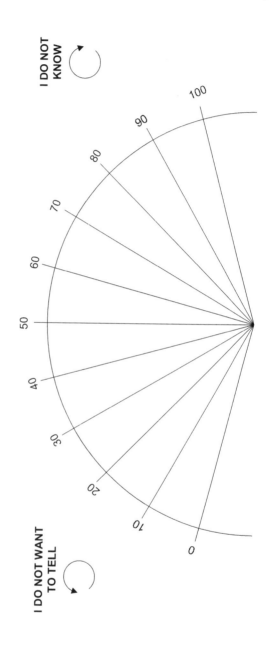

CHART "0 to 100"

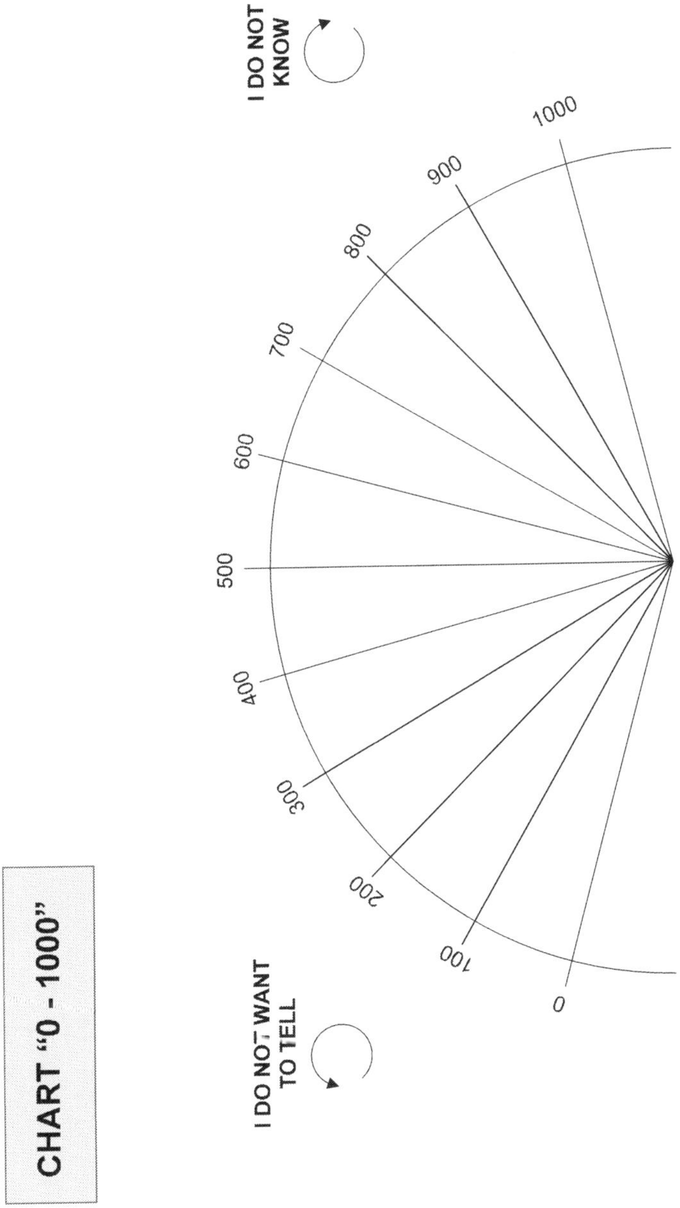

**119**

I DO NOT KNOW ↻

1000
900
800
700
600
500
400
300
200
100
0

I DO NOT WANT TO TELL ↻

CHART "0 - 1000"

**CHART "0 to 1000"**

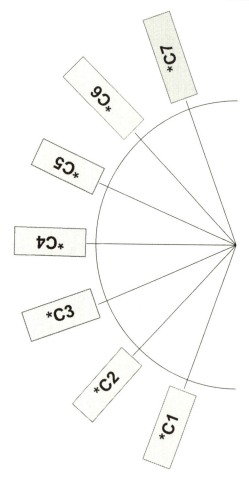

## CHART C1.
## What Needs Attention

*C1. Health conditions.
*C2. Circumstances.
*C3. Situations.
*C4. Influences.
*C5. Finances.
*C6. Job situation
*C7. Go to "CHART S1"

**CHART C1. What Needs Attention**

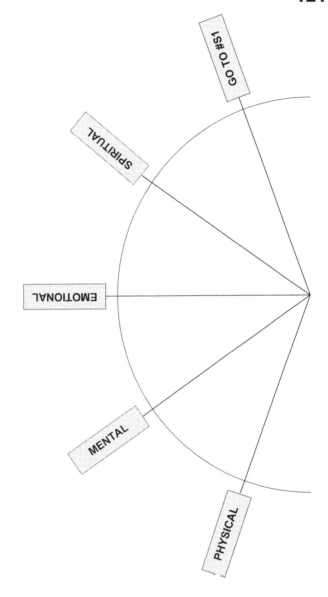

CHART C1a. Main Areas of Life

**122**

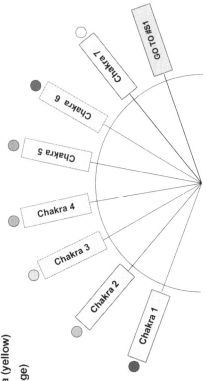

**CHART C1b.
Chakras.**

Chakra # 7 – Crown Chakra (white)
Chakra # 6 – Third-Eye-Chakra (indigo)
Chakra # 5 – Throat Chakra (blue)
Chakra # 4 – Heart Chakra (green)
Chakra # 3 – Solar Plexus Chakra (yellow)
Chakra # 2 – Sacral Chakra (orange)
Chakra # 1 – Root Chakra (red)

*CHART C1b. Chakras*

# CHART C2. FINDINGS
## Severity of a Condition or Situation

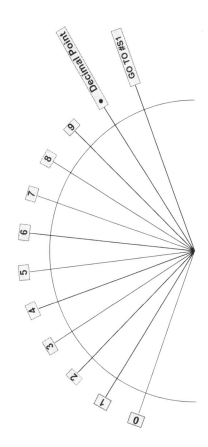

**Severity of Situation or Condition:**
0. Very severe condition, needs an urgent intervention
1. Significant problem, needs quick intervention
2. Medium problem, needs intervention, no rush
3. Some minor problems, may go away on its own
4. Needs attention, problems may develop in a month
5. Borderline, but OK
6. Behaving properly
7. Good condition
8. Very good condition
9. Excellent condition

*CHART C2. Severity of a Condition or Situation*

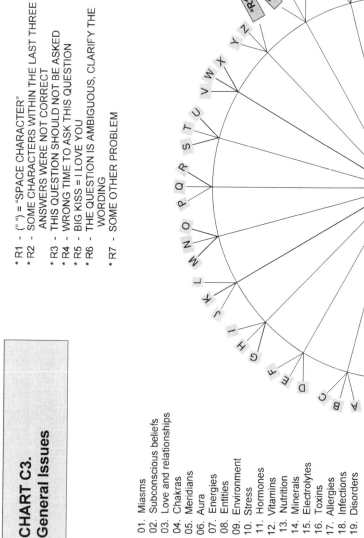

## CHART C3.
## General Issues

- **A.** 01. Miasms
- **B.** 02. Subconscious beliefs
- **C.** 03. Love and relationships
- **D.** 04. Chakras
- **E.** 05. Meridians
- **F.** 06. Aura
- **G.** 07. Energies
- **H.** 08. Entities
- **I.** 09. Environment
- **J.** 10. Stress
- **K.** 11. Hormones
- **L.** 12. Vitamins
- **M.** 13. Nutrition
- **N.** 14. Minerals
- **O.** 15. Electrolytes
- **P.** 16. Toxins
- **Q.** 17. Allergies
- **R.** 18. Infections
- **R.** 19. Disorders

* R1 - (" ") = "SPACE CHARACTER"
* R2 - SOME CHARACTERS WITHIN THE LAST THREE ANSWERS WERE NOT CORRECT
* R3 - THIS QUESTION SHOULD NOT BE ASKED
* R4 - WRONG TIME TO ASK THIS QUESTION
* R5 - BIG KISS = I LOVE YOU
* R6 - THE QUESTION IS AMBIGUOUS, CLARIFY THE WORDING
* R7 - SOME OTHER PROBLEM

*CHART C3. General Issues*

## CHART C4.
## Body Systems

A. Digestive system
B. Respiratory system
C. Urinary system
D. Female reproductive system
E. Male reproductive system
F. Endocrine glands
G. Circulatory system
H. Lymphatic system
I. Nervous system
J. Peripheral nervous system
K. Sensory organs
L. Integumentary system (skin and its appendages)
M. Other body systems (skeleton, muscles etc.).

* R1 - (" ") = "SPACE CHARACTER"
* R2 - SOME CHARACTERS WITHIN THE LAST THREE ANSWERS WERE NOT CORRECT
* R3 - THIS QUESTION SHOULD NOT BE ASKED
* R4 - WRONG TIME TO ASK THIS QUESTION
* R5 - BIG KISS = I LOVE YOU
* R6 - THE QUESTION IS AMBIGUOUS, CLARIFY THE WORDING
* R7 - SOME OTHER PROBLEM

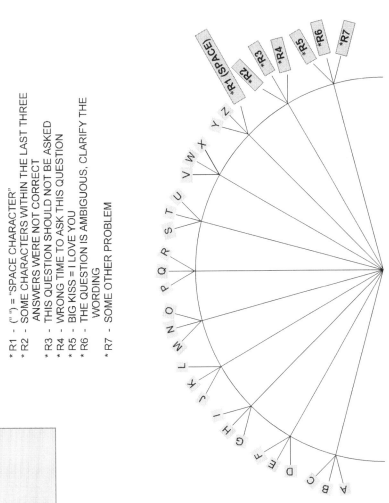

*CHART C4. Body Systems*

**CHART C5.**
**Categories of Bach Flower Remedies**

Category 1 - Fear
Category 2 - Uncertainty
Category 3 - Disinterest in Current Circumstances
Category 4 - Loneliness
Category 5 - Oversensitivity to Ideas
Category 6 - Loss of Hope and Despair
Category 7 - Overly concerned about Others' Welfare

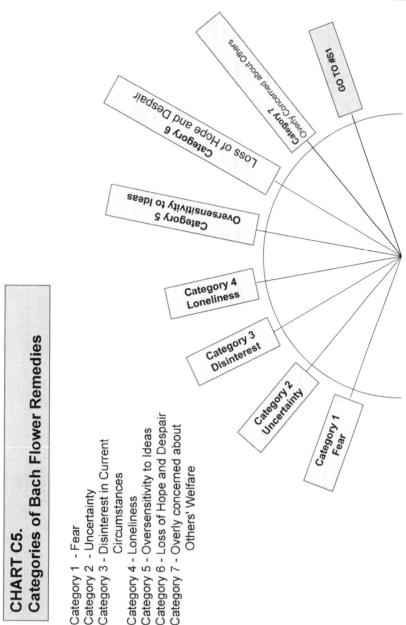

*CHART C5. Categories of Bach Flower Remedies*

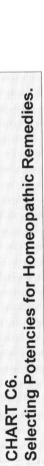
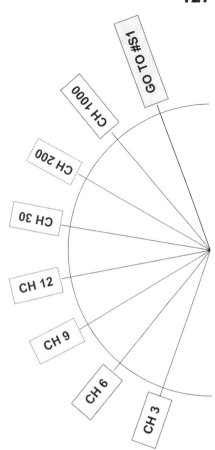

*CHART C6. Selecting Potencies in Homeopathy*

**128**

## CHART C7.
### Number of Days to the Next Remedy.

=================
Remedy 1: ........
Potency: ........
=================
Remedy 2: ........
Potency: ........
=================
Remedy 2: ........
Potency: ........
=================

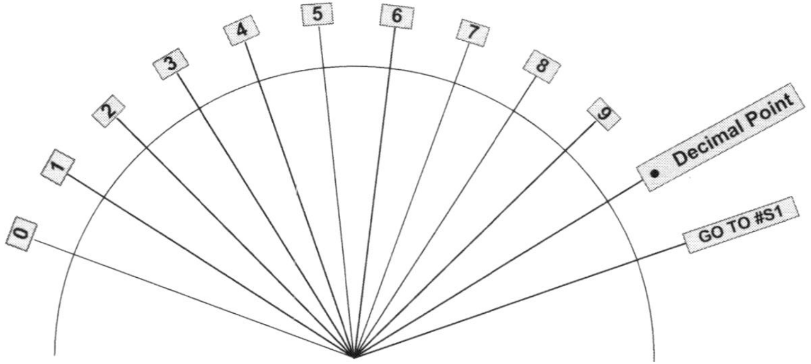

Pendulum chart with numbers 0–9, Decimal Point, and GO TO #S1.

Use this chart to plan the time-gaps between taking the homeopathic remedies. To get the numbers, first ask the pendulum if the reading should be for two digits. Use the Schedule-Calendar from the Appendix C for planning.

## *CHART C7. Number of Days to the Next Remedy.*

Made in the USA
San Bernardino, CA
01 August 2018